Lye, Keith

Take a trip to Yugoslavia

DATE DUE

Pulled X

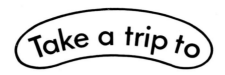

YUGOSLAVIA

Keith Lye
General Editor
Henry Pluckrose

Franklin Watts

London   New York   Sydney   Toronto

Facts about Yugoslavia

Area:
255,804 sq. km.
(98,766 sq. miles)

Population:
22,777,000

Capital:
Belgrade

Largest cities:
Belgrade (1,407,000)
Zagreb (1,175,000)
Skopje (507,000)
Sarajevo (448,000)
Ljubljana (305,000)

Official languages:
Serbo-Croat, Slovenian,
Macedonian

Religions:
Christianity, Islam

Main exports:
Machinery, electrical
goods, transport equip-
ment, other manufactures,
chemicals

Currency:
Dinar

Franklin Watts
12a Golden Square
London W1

Franklin Watts Inc.
387 Park Avenue South
New York, N.Y. 10016

ISBN: UK Edition 0 86 313 499 8
ISBN: US Edition 0 531 10289 0
Library of Congress Catalog Card No:
86 50899

© Franklin Watts Limited 1987

Typeset by Ace Filmsetting Ltd
Frome, Somerset
Printed in Hong Kong

Maps: Susan Kinsey and Simon
Roulestone
Design: Edward Kinsey

Stamps: Stanley Gibbons Limited
Photographs: J. Allan Cash 3, 15, 16, 17,
22, 23, 24, 25; Paul Forrester 12;
Yugoslavian Airlines 5; Yugoslav
National Tourist Office 4, 6, 9, 19, 21, 28,
30, 31; ZEFA 7, 8, 10, 14, 18, 20, 26, 27,
29

Front Cover: ZEFA
Back Cover: Yugoslav National Tourist
Board

Yugoslavia, a country in southern
Europe, borders the Adriatic Sea.
Many islands lie off the coast,
including Hvar, shown above.
Yugoslavia first became a country in
1918. Its present name meaning
"Land of the Southern Slavs" was
adopted in 1929. Slavs are people
who speak similar languages and live
mostly in eastern Europe.

3

Yugoslavia has six main Slavic groups: the Serbs, Croats, Bosnian Muslims, Slovenes, Macedonians and Montenegrins. Belgrade, the national capital, is peopled mainly by Serbs. Some 18 other groups, including Albanians and Hungarians, make up 15 percent of Yugoslavia's population.

Because of its varied population, Yugoslavia is divided into six republics: Bosnia-Hercegovina, Croatia, Macedonia, Montenegro, Serbia and Slovenia. Each republic has its own government. The Federal Assembly (parliament) is in Belgrade, which is also the capital of Serbia.

Zagreb, Yugoslavia's second largest city, is capital of Croatia. The Croatians and the Serbs speak a language called Serbo-Croat. This is one of Yugoslavia's three official languages.

6

Skopje is the capital of Macedonia, in southeastern Yugoslavia. It is on the Vardar River. Macedonian is also an official language in Yugoslavia. An earthquake destroyed much of Skopje in 1963, but it has been rebuilt.

Sarajevo is the capital of Bosnia-Hercegovina, in central Yugoslavia. Bosnian Muslims make up about 40 percent of the population of Bosnia-Hercegovina. Most of the others are Croatians or Serbs.

8

Ljubljana is the capital of the republic of Slovenia, in northern Yugoslavia. It is on the Ljubljanica River, a tributary of the Sava River. Slovenian is one of the three official languages in Yugoslavia.

The republic of Montenegro in the southwest is largely mountainous, with some large forests. Most Montenegrins speak Serbo-Croat. The capital of Montenegro is Titograd, a town named after President Tito, a leader of the resistance in World War II. Tito later became his country's leader.

In 1945, President Tito set up a Communist republic, now officially called the Socialist Federal Republic of Yugoslavia. At first, he allied his country with Russia. Yugoslavia broke with Russia in 1948, but it remained a Communist country. Tito died in 1980, but his picture is often displayed.

The picture shows some stamps and money used in Yugoslavia. The main unit of currency is the dinar, which is divided into 100 paras.

Yugoslavia

AUSTRIA

HUNGARY

R. Danube

Piran ● ●Maribor
●Ljubljana

Pannonian Plains

●Rijeka ●Zagreb

Subotica

ROMANIA

R. Sava

Novi Sad

Banja Luka●

Belgrade

YUGOSLAVIA

R. Moravia

Sarajevo
●Split

Kragujevac●

●Mostar

Nis●

Hvar

●Dubrovnik

BULGARIA

Titograd●

Urosevac

ITALY

Adriatic Sea

●Skopje

ALBANIA GREECE

13

Yugoslavia has three main land regions. The narrow coastlands, with their hot, dry summers and mild winters, contain tourist resorts, such as Split. Parts of the walls of the ruined Roman Palace of Diocletian in Split can be seen in this picture.

Behind the coastlands are rugged mountain ranges. The highest mountains are the Julian Alps in the northwest, which reach 2,863 metres (9,393 ft). They have much colder winters than the coast. Many ski resorts are found in the Julian Alps.

The Pannonian plains in the northeast include Yugoslavia's best farmland. Major rivers are the Sava, Drava and Danube. They often flood when heavy rains occur in spring or autumn. Summers are hot and dry here, but winters are cold.

Crops are grown on 44 percent of the land. In most Communist countries, the government owns most of the land. But in Yugoslavia, 83 percent of the farmland is privately owned. Corn, sugar beet and wheat are produced on the Pannonian plains.

Agriculture employs 29 percent of the country's work force. Grapes, grown mainly for wine, other fruits and olives are major crops on the coast. Yugoslavia is tenth among the world's top wine producers.

The mountain grasslands provide excellent pasture for Yugoslavia's seven or eight million sheep. The country also has more than five million cattle, over eight million pigs and 70 million poultry.

Piran lies on the coast near the head of the Adriatic Sea. In the 1980s, Yugoslavia's fishing fleet contained more than 1,100 sailing or rowing boats and 220 motor-driven vessels.

Forests cover more than 40 percent of Yugoslavia. Beech, fir and oak are the chief trees. The forests in this picture are in the republic of Montenegro. Much of the timber is used in building and for furniture.

Industries employ 35 percent of the work force. Minerals include bauxite, chrome ore, coal, copper, iron and lead. The main industrial areas are in the northeast. The government owns and runs most factories.

Leading industrial products include steel, cement, chemicals, plastics and textiles. There are also many craft industries. Turkish carpets are made in Mostar, in Bosnia-Hercegovina, a region once ruled by Turkey.

Education is free at all levels in Yugoslavia. Children must attend school for at least eight years. Pupils then go on to vocational or secondary schools for three to four years. Because of Yugoslavia's many languages, most people speak at least two languages.

Pupils are taught in their own language. This means that there are schools using not only Slavic languages, such as Serbo-Croat, the most widely spoken language, but also minority languages, including Albanian, Czech, Hungarian, Italian, Romanian, Turkish and Ukrainian.

Many country people, like this family in Croatia, live in small houses made of wood or stone, while most city people live in apartment buildings. Living standards are generally high.

Shops and markets, like this one in Dubrovnik on the coast, have a wide range of goods. Popular foods vary from region to region. Grilled meats, stuffed vine leaves and stuffed green peppers are common dishes.

About a third of Yugoslavia's people belong to the Eastern Orthodox Church, including many Macedonians, Montenegrins and Serbians. This monastery is in central Serbia. Roman Catholics make up a quarter of the population, including many Croats and Slovenes.

About a tenth of the people of
Yugoslavia are Muslims. The
Muslim religion, Islam, is commonest
in the south, which was once ruled by
Turkey. The mosque in this picture is
at Urosevac in southwestern Serbia.
Some Protestants and Jews also live
in the country.

Yachting, swimming and fishing are popular pastimes on the coast. Soccer is the leading team game, while many people enjoy meeting their friends in coffee houses.

Yugoslavia's many national groups preserve their culture, including traditional costumes, dances, songs and handicrafts. These dancers live in Slovenia.

31

Index

HEADS, I WIN

Also by Patricia Hermes

FRIENDS ARE LIKE THAT

WHO WILL TAKE CARE OF ME?

YOU SHOULDN'T HAVE TO SAY GOOD-BYE

NOBODY'S FAULT?

WHAT IF THEY KNEW?

KEVIN CORBETT EATS FLIES

A PLACE FOR JEREMY

for young adults

A SOLITARY SECRET

nonfiction

A TIME TO LISTEN

HEADS, I WIN

by Patricia Hermes

ILLUSTRATED BY CAROL NEWSOM

HARCOURT BRACE JOVANOVICH, PUBLISHERS

SAN DIEGO   NEW YORK   LONDON

HBJ

Text copyright © 1988 by Patricia Hermes
Illustrations copyright © 1988 by Carol Newsom

Requests for permission to make copies of any
part of the work should be mailed to:
Permissions, Harcourt Brace Jovanovich, Publishers,
Orlando, Florida 32887.

Library of Congress Cataloging-in-Publication Data
Hermes, Patricia.
Heads, I win.
Summary: In this sequel to "Kevin Corbett Eats Flies,"
Bailey runs for class president hoping that popularity
will secure her place in her current foster home.
[1. Foster home care—Fiction.   2. Elections—Fiction.
3. Schools—Fiction]   I. Newsom, Carol, ill.   II. Title.
PZ7.H4317He   1988   [Fic]   87-19249

ISBN 0-15-233659-1

Design by Camilla Filancia,
based on a design by Julie Durrell
Printed in the United States of America

First edition

A B C D E

For my son

Matthew Hermes

with love

List of Illustrations

HEADS, I WIN

I WAS STUCK—in this dumb, boring classroom with dumb, boring Janie reading her dumb essay called "Time Pilot." I had to do something about it. But what?

Every time Janie started a new sentence, she rocked up on her toes and then down. I'd been counting. She'd done it twenty-seven times. Twenty-seven sentences. Watching her made me feel seasick. If only she felt seasick, too, and then threw up all over, that would liven things up.

On and on Janie droned, up on her toes and down. Janie's face gets real red whenever Miss Holt calls on her to give a report. Then, when she starts speaking, she gets so pale that she looks as if she's going to puke. You can tell she hates to give reports, so I can't figure out why she does such long ones—unless it's because the more you talk, the better grade teachers give you.

Janie's real stuck-up. She hasn't spoken to me since I started in this school last fall, but every time I walk by her and her friends, Stephanie and Violet, they all start whispering together. Like this morning, all three of them leaned away from me when I walked by. Janie made a big thing of holding her hand over her nose till I was past. I don't smell. I don't get all dressed up the way they do because—well, just because. School is not a beauty contest. But I am clean.

Janie was still going on. Thirty-four ups and downs now. Thirty-four sentences. This could go in *The Guinness Book of World Records* for the longest fifth-grade essay.

Two aisles over, Kevin and Brant were playing a game of desk football. Kevin Corbett is practically the only kid in the class who's not either boring or stuck-up. And he's my friend—my really good friend. He tries to ignore me in school because I'm a girl, but he's nice to me outside school. I told him one day it was in school *and* out—or nothing. I could tell he was scared half to death—probably of what the guys would say—but he finally agreed. Still, we don't hang around together on the school playground. But I can tell he's not quite so scared about being my friend in class anymore.

Like this morning, he walked by just when Janie was doing that nose-holding thing. I don't know if he knew she was doing it because of me, but he said to her, real loud, "Do you stink, Janie? Did you wet your bed last night?" And she got all red.

Kevin's cool. He's got that kind of dark brown hair that's real shiny, so when you see him in the sunlight, his hair has a sort of circle of light in it. But he's a real show-off, too. In class, as soon as the teacher's not looking, he does show-off stuff—like swallowing flies and spiders. His friend Brant used to bring them to him, and people actually paid Kevin to swallow them. Five cents for flies, ten cents for spiders.

Anybody can swallow flies and spiders. You don't even have to taste them if you put them far enough back on your tongue. I know—I've tried it. But it takes talent to do the trick I do. I learned it from this street person, Jessica, who spends a lot of time on Spruce Street. Jessica taught me to aim with a rubber band, and if you do it right, you can snap flies right off a windowsill or a desk or something. I'm working now on snapping flies out of the air, but that's a little harder.

Now Kevin was making a goalpost with his fingers, and Brant was trying to snip a paper football through them. They kept looking to see if Miss Holt saw them, but she was watching Janie as if she were hypnotized. Maybe she was counting Janie's going up and down, too. Or maybe she was asleep with her eyes open. I've heard that some people can do that.

Stephanie and Violet were passing Garbage Pail Kid cards under the desks to each other. And Owen was drawing airplanes with streaks of fire coming out of them all over the cover of his spelling book.

I had an idea. I picked up my pen. In big letters, across the back of my hand, I wrote: B-O-R-I-N-G. Then I propped my hand under my chin so that Miss Holt would have to see. She didn't even blink, just kept her eyes on Janie. I bet she *was* asleep!

Rats. I had to find some way to keep from dying of boredom. I'd read somewhere that people really can die from that. What to do?

I shifted my books toward the corner of my desk. I could let them all drop on the floor at the same time.

Or I could hold my breath and press on that certain spot on my neck and try to faint.

Or I could burp real loud. I'm pretty good at it. I can do one that comes out with a good roar and then sort of rolls along with little bounces. Besides, I was chewing bubble gum now, and that always helps make a good burp.

Or I could do that thing that the music teacher in my other school used to make us do—this voice exercise. We had to open our mouths real wide, then roll our tongues down behind our bottom front teeth, and try to make a breathing sound from the back of our throats. When you make the sound, it sort of makes your tongue thrust out, and you look and sound like some weird monster. I found that if, at the same time you're making that sound, you roll your eyes way back so you can see only the white part, then you look and sound not only weird, but *really* scary.

I could do that. Except that the kids might think I actually was weird, or was having a fit or something. Not that I cared that much.

Suddenly I had an idea. Brilliant. It might still be boring, but I'd get a laugh. And I'd sure get even with Janie.

I tore a little piece of paper off my notebook and wrote a note that said, "Watch what happens," and put Kevin's name on it. Then I passed it to Jennifer, who was sitting next to me. I can't tell whether Jennifer likes me or not. She doesn't say much. And when she does, she blushes and sort of rolls her eyes up. But she took the note.

When she saw Kevin's name on it, she put it on the corner of her desk nearest him.

Kevin reached over and snatched it off. I saw him open it under his desk, read it, and then pass it to Brant.

I waited till Janie was all finished. Miss Holt blinked a couple of times as if she were coming out of a trance. Then she said, "Thank you, Janie. That was very well done."

That's when I raised my hand.

"Yes, Bailey?" Miss Holt said.

"Not to be mean or anything," I said, "but I didn't understand anything Janie said."

Miss Holt looked kind of dumbfounded. "Oh," she

said. I don't think she thought for a minute that anyone was actually paying attention.

I tried to look very serious.

"Oh," Miss Holt said again. Then she said, "Would you like to ask Janie to explain anything?"

I could feel everyone in the class watching me. "I just think maybe if Janie did it all over again—but more slowly this time—then I'd understand it," I said. "See, I really would like to know more about time travel."

"No!" Janie practically shouted it. "No, Miss Holt! I did it already!" She had gotten real red again.

Everybody started talking at the same time.

"No, Miss Holt!" Violet said. "Please? We already *heard* it." She dragged out the word "heard" like this: *hurrrrrrrrrrrrrrd.*

Miss Holt said, "Well, Bailey. I—I—I just don't know . . . "

I could tell she was horrified at the thought of listening to Janie again, but she didn't know how to get out of it.

It was really hard not to laugh. But I kept my most serious face on.

"Miss Holt!" It was Kevin, shouting above all the noise.

I didn't turn to look at him, but I watched him out of the corner of my eye.

"Miss Holt!" Kevin said again.

The whole class quieted down. I think Kevin would be a better teacher than Miss Holt is. I don't know why, but everybody pays attention to him.

"I think Bailey's right," Kevin said when the room got quiet. He looked dead serious. "I think we should hear it again."

I laughed right out loud, tried to cover it up by

5

coughing, and almost swallowed my bubble gum. I coughed and coughed and practically choked before I got the gum back up out of my throat. Jennifer reached over and punched me on the back.

Lots of people were groaning, but not as many as before. Practically everybody wants to be on Kevin's side.

Miss Holt looked from Kevin to me and then back again. You could almost see her trying to decide how to get out of it. Then she got that look that teachers do sometimes—that super-bright smile that means they think they've come up with a bright idea.

"I know," she said. "How about if we have an early morning recess today? Bailey and Kevin and anyone else who has questions can talk to Janie on the playground. I'll give you an extra-long recess to do it."

"Yeah! Yeah!" Everybody was shouting.

"And then when you come back in," Miss Holt added above all the shouting, "I have some exciting news for you."

Nobody paid any attention to that. Exciting news for a teacher usually means she's picking a new person to change the paper in the hamster's cage or something.

There was a scramble for the coat closet to get sweaters and balls and stuff for the playground.

Janie glared at me, but I just smiled back sweetly.

I got up and stood close to Kevin. I wanted to say, "Thanks," but I couldn't. I hoped he'd say something. But even though it took him a while to get his Nerf football and stuff together, he left without saying anything to me, either.

Everybody went outside then. I really didn't have anyone to talk to on the playground, so I went to the lavatory instead. I looked all around and under the stalls to make sure no one was there. Then I pulled up my sweatshirt and stuck my head into my armpit. I didn't smell. I knew it.

I stood in front of the mirror and practiced two things I might need this afternoon if things kept on being this boring—blowing bubbles and burping. While I was doing that, I was thinking about my foster homes—the last one and this new one. My last foster mom, Mrs. Hughes, the cat lady, seemed like a fairy godmother compared to this new one. Except I knew Mrs. Hughes wanted to get rid of me, so I had made up an excuse to leave first. It wasn't just an excuse—it was true. I was sick of living with her yowly cats. Thirty-three of them. Each one had a name, and sometimes she called me by one of the cat's names. So one day I locked myself in my room (my *green* room— she loved green, everything in that house was green) and told her I was allergic to her dumb cats, and I wouldn't come out until the social worker came to see for herself how allergic I was. I had found out that if you put a bobby pin in your nose and wriggle it around kind of gently, it makes you sneeze lots. But you have to be sure to pull out the bobby pin before the sneeze comes, or it jabs right up into your brain. So when the social worker got there, I stayed behind my locked door with the bobby pin in my nose and sneezed about a thousand times while she stood out in the hall, begging me to come out. I told her I'd come out only if she'd put me somewhere else.

So now I was with Ms. Henderson, who didn't have any cats. But she didn't have anything else, either, like brains, or a heart. I almost laughed out loud at that thought. It sounded like the Scarecrow and the Tin Woodman in *The Wizard of Oz*. Not that I wanted Ms. Henderson to *love* me or anything. I didn't. I'd die if she was mushy or anything. But at least she could notice me. I think half the time she doesn't even know I'm there.

Every so often she just looks up at me with that vague kind of look, as if she's surprised to see me there. Actually, I can get away with a lot with her not paying much attention to me, so I guess it's better this way. And she's not mean to me or anything. But I am always stuck with baby-sitting her kid, Matthew. Probably that's why she got me—to have a live-in baby-sitter. And I was stuck in this stupid school, with these stupid, stuck-up kids. Except for Kevin, my one good friend.

But I'd show those stuck-up girls—especially Janie, the leader of the pack. I leaned closer to the mirror and practiced blowing more bubbles. I blew one really huge, enormous one, but it burst, and I had to unglue it from my face and hair and even from the mirror. It was a pretty gross job, but I had to do it, not only to get it off me, but also because it was my last piece of gum.

It was hard work picking the strands out of my eyelashes without poking my eyes out. I have long eyelashes and green eyes. My eyes are the only good part about my face—at least, that's what Mrs. Hughes always used to say. "You're a skinny waif," she always said. "But those eyes make up for a lot." She probably liked them only because they were green.

The bathroom door banged open. In the mirror, I could see Stephanie and Violet and Janie come trooping in, holding the door open for someone behind them. They stopped dead still when they saw me. Then they looked at each other, and all three of them laughed out loud.

Behind them, I saw Jennifer standing in the doorway. She looked at everybody, then ducked her head like she was embarrassed, and fled into a stall and slammed the door.

I shrugged as if I didn't care and just kept picking strands of bubble gum off the mirror like this was what I always did at recess time. I yanked hard at the bubble gum strands, pretending it was hair I was pulling out of Janie's stupid head.

And the whole time I was thinking of some way to show them. I was as good as they were, and I'd prove it. They'd see. I didn't know yet what I'd do. But I knew I'd think of something.

2

As soon as we got back to class after recess, Miss Holt sprang something on us.

"Boys and girls," she said as soon as we were seated. "At the faculty meeting after school yesterday, a decision was made. Something we teachers are very excited about."

She paused and beamed at us.

I rolled my eyes.

"Something that I believe *you'll* find exciting, too," Miss Holt went on.

Don't count on it, I thought.

I looked at Kevin. He rolled his eyes, too. That's what I like about him—he thinks the same as I do.

Some of the other kids started getting interested. There was a whole chorus of "What's exciting, Miss Holt? What?"

"We're going to have elections," Miss Holt said. "For"—she paused dramatically—"class president!" She used the same kind of voice that the person uses who does the Miss America announcements.

A couple kids went, "Yeah!" But there were a lot of groans, too.

"And then," Miss Holt went on, ignoring the groaning, "all the class presidents will be members of a student

10

council. And the student council will help to run the school."

She smiled at us as if she had just announced that school would be closed for the rest of the year. She has a nice smile—for a teacher. And she's even kind of pretty. What's gross is that all the girls copy her, the way she dresses, and her hair and everything. Janie's the worst, the biggest copycat. And whatever Janie does, everybody else does. So Miss Holt has long, long bangs that practically cover her eyes, and so does every girl in the class— except me. I think they all look like sheep dogs.

A lot of kids seemed to think running for president was exciting, probably because they thought they could really get a chance to run the school. But I knew better. Grown-ups would never let kids run a school—or anything else, for that matter.

Everybody was talking at the same time. Miss Holt always tells us to raise our hands when we want to talk, but nobody does—everyone just shouts at once, and Miss Holt tries to answer everyone at once. Yet I've noticed that if you really want attention and raise your hand, Miss Holt calls on you. I don't know why nobody else has discovered that.

Owen wiped his nose on his sleeve. "Miss Holt!" he shouted out. "Will the kids *really* have a say in running the school?"

Owen's nose is always stuffed up, so what he actually said was "Will duh kith weally have a thay id wuddig duh thkool?"

"Really," Miss Holt said.

I saw Janie pull out a notebook.

I knew exactly what she was doing—planning her campaign for president.

"Like how?" Brant asked. "What would they do?"

11

Brant's a little kid, smaller than anyone else in the fifth grade. Even smaller than me. But he's pretty cool—even though he's in love with Miss Holt, and he doesn't try to hide it.

"Well, that will be decided as we go along," Miss Holt said.

I'll bet, I thought. But I decided to test it. I raised my hand.

"Yes, Bailey?"

"Will the student council get to decide if we have homework on weekends or not?" I asked.

Everybody looked first at me and then at Miss Holt.

"I'm not sure," she said doubtfully. "I think that's probably something each individual teacher would decide."

I knew it. They'd never let kids decide anything important. I pulled out a piece of paper and my origami book. Everybody else could try to be class president. Not me.

Carefully, I folded over a corner of my paper, thinking about the pattern I wanted. I'd gotten the origami book from the art teacher, and I liked doing this stuff.

Miss Holt spoke again. "The student council *will* decide certain important things, though," she said. "Such things as appropriate rewards and punishments for certain kinds of behavior."

Big deal. I kept on folding my paper.

"And," she went on, "of course the meetings will be held during schooltime."

I looked up.

She was looking right at me. She does that a lot, as if she's trying to figure me out. It's not a mean look or anything, just a sort of wondering look. I like that—I mean, that she doesn't know what's going on with me. It's always good to keep teachers guessing.

"So," she went on. "If you were a council member, you'd attend a meeting at least once a week. There'd probably be other events that would cut into class time. So whoever's elected would have to be a good student. A good speaker, too, because you'd have to give lots of reports to the classes. And that's why anyone who runs for president will have to make a campaign speech."

That started everybody shouting out questions again. It seemed like Miss Holt just kept looking at me. But this time it wasn't a questioning look. It was more like a— a challenge, maybe? A dare? But how come?

I took a deep breath and thought about it. I was a good student, or I could be if I felt like it. So I could be on a student council that would run the school. Of course, it wouldn't really. But it would mean I'd be getting out of class. And besides . . .

I couldn't help feeling at least a little interested. If I could get elected, it might be a way . . . a way to show those stuck-up girls. Especially with Janie over there already planning her campaign.

Still, I didn't know why Miss Holt seemed to be encouraging *me* to run for class president. Unless it wasn't really me she wanted. I've noticed that some teachers try to get on the good side of you when they want your help. That's probably what it was. She probably wanted me to help her persuade the other kids that it was a good idea.

"Good student?" Violet yelled. "How good?"

"Could you help me after school, Miss Holt?" Brant shouted.

"Does that mean all *A*'s, Miss Holt?" Janie said. " 'Cause if it does, I'm president automatically! I'm straight *A*'s. And I'd be great at campaign speeches."

Yeah, I thought. *Long, boring ones.*

But for once Miss Holt wasn't trying to answer all

the kids at once. She still seemed to be looking directly at me.

I made a decision. *Okay, I'll do it.* I looked away.

I put away the origami book and the paper that I was about to fold. So I was definitely going to run for class president. School president, too. President of the world, if it would help keep me out of class. And for that other reason: If I could really win, could really be president of the class, that would be one way to show them that I am as good as they are.

If anyone would vote for me. Yeah, they would. I'd make them. I'd find a way.

It was time to begin thinking of a campaign.

The class was really in an uproar by then. All the kids had gotten out of their seats and were now bunched up around Miss Holt's desk. All but Kevin and me—and Janie, who was bent over her desk on the other side of Kevin, already at work on her campaign.

I turned to Kevin. "Want to be my campaign manager?" I asked.

"*Yours?*" he said. "No."

"Why not?"

"Because I was going to ask you the same thing," he said.

"Oh."

This was dumb. I needed Kevin. And knowing him, he wouldn't give in easily.

We just sat there staring at each other.

I sighed. I needed him. He was really my only friend, so far. Unless—could I ask Jennifer? Or Brant? But I wanted Kevin!

"You sure?" I said.

He nodded. "Yup. You?"

I nodded.

I saw that Janie had looked up from her book and was watching Kevin and me, listening to every word.

The minute I looked at her, she raised her hand. "Miss Holt!" she yelled. "Miss Holt? Can just anybody run? I mean—even *new* people?" She crinkled up her nose when she said the word "new," like she was really saying "throw-up."

Miss Holt didn't answer. Janie probably hadn't even been heard above all the uproar. But Kevin and I both heard her.

And Kevin answered, real loud, "It's a *democracy,* Janie! Anyone can run! Even you."

"But Bailey doesn't *know* anybody!" Janie said. "Or anything about the school." She gave me the same kind of look Mrs. Hughes used when she saw a cockroach on the kitchen wall at night. She added, "And we don't know anything about her, either."

"Stuff it, Janie," Kevin said. He turned his back to her and faced me. "Okay," he said quietly.

"Okay, what?"

"Okay I'll be your campaign manager."

I squinted, suddenly suspicious. He wasn't doing this because he felt sorry for me, was he?

"Why?" I said.

"*Why?* What are you—weird?"

I looked at him hard. He didn't seem to be feeling sorry for me. But he did look kind of mad because I hadn't said yes right away.

"So?" he said. "You want to or not?"

"Yeah."

"Okay, then."

For the second time that day, I wanted to say thanks and didn't.

"Now," Kevin said. "You need a campaign. Something terrific." He sucked on the new wire that he's just gotten across his front teeth. It's not braces, but a thing called a retainer. He can pop it in and out when he wants to. "But what?" he said.

I'd already been thinking. I looked around the class. "There's twenty-six kids in this class, right?" I said.

Kevin nodded.

"And half of them will run for president, right?"

He looked at the mob around Miss Holt's desk. "Prob'ly," he said.

"So that means they'll each vote for themselves, right?"

"Definitely," he said. He worked his lips around the retainer. Then he ran his tongue over his teeth, popped out the retainer, and shoved it into his pocket.

I watched him enviously. I wished I had a retainer. When you pop it out, it looks really gross—a wire attached to a pink plastic thing that runs across the roof of your mouth. I could pop it out at Janie.

"So," I said, "if we can get even a couple kids not to run, then we get their votes. And I win!"

"So how do we persuade anybody not to run?" Kevin asked. "And even if we get them not to run, how do we get them to vote for you?"

I looked up. Janie was practically falling out of her chair from trying so hard to hear what we were saying.

I leaned over and whispered something in Kevin's ear.

His eyes opened wide, and he laughed. "You can get in trouble for that," he said. He took the retainer out of his pocket, blew some pocket fuzzies off it, and worked it back into his mouth.

"Nah," I said. "Not really. So what do you think?"

He shook his head, but he laughed again. I could tell that he liked my idea. "Why not?" he said.

He took out a notebook and turned to a fresh page. And across the top of the page, in big letters, he wrote: "Bailey for President!"

The campaign was beginning.

3

I HUNG AROUND for a long time after school that day, going over my plan with Kevin. We talked for so long that it was getting dark by the time I left him. I raced home as fast as my old bike would go. It was almost time for Ms. Henderson to leave for work and for me to baby-sit Matt. He's only four years old, and she works nights, so I take care of him. He's really not a bad little kid, plus she pays me for it.

I hoped we'd have our lights back on. Three days ago, the electric company had turned off the electricity because Ms. Henderson hadn't paid the bill. The first day it was fun, doing everything with candles and flashlights. Then it got to be a pain, taking care of Matt and doing homework in the dark. There was no TV for Matt to watch, so he was really cranky. I don't think it happened because Ms. Henderson is too poor to pay her bills, although she does say she has trouble making ends meet. I think she forgets to pay bills sometimes, the same way she's forgetful about money. But as soon as I got home that first day the electricity went off, she gave me money, and I took it to the 7-Eleven to get a money order made out to the electric company. Then I mailed the payment in.

Outside, the streetlights came on just as I came around my corner. As I rode under the light, I could see my shadow riding beside me, and then, as I passed the light, my shadow slid behind me. I looked over my shoulder and saw that my bike wheels looked enormous and that I had gotten long and tall. I was so busy looking that I almost rammed a car parked at the curb, right in front of Ms. Henderson's house. I swerved just in time to avoid it. Good thing, too. People get really mad if you bang into their cars, even if their cars are pretty ugly.

This car was ugly, too—brown and fat. Who would buy a brown car? Probably someone like Owen when he grew up. Then I saw the little round seal on the side door—the State of Connecticut seal. A state car. Someone from the Welfare Department? A social worker?

I stopped beside the car, feeling my heart banging hard against my chest. I looked up at the house. Had Ms. Henderson decided to get rid of me—just like Mrs. Hughes had been wanting to? But the apartment was perfectly dark, as though no one lived there at all.

I peeked inside the car. They wouldn't have moved me out already, would they? Packed up my stuff and put it in the car? No, there was only the usual junk in the car—clipboards, papers, a lunch or something in a brown paper bag. A coffee cup.

What to do? Nobody ever got rid of me. I left them first. If the social worker was here, should I tell her I wanted to leave, that I was sick of Ms. Henderson forgetting to pay her bills, sick of living in the dark? But I *didn't* want to leave.

For one crazy minute, I thought of running away— hiding somewhere till after the elections. But I knew that was dumb. I had to go upstairs right now and find out what was happening.

I checked the mailbox by the curb. A bunch of ads and a bill. I parked my bike under the steps and locked it, then slowly climbed the stairs. I stepped over the broken fourth step, and then skipped the eighth one, too—my lucky way of coming in. But I didn't feel lucky. My legs felt rubbery, the way they do when I get scared.

It was dark at the top of the stairs, and when I opened the apartment door, it was still dark—pitch dark inside, although I saw the gleam of a flashlight or a candle from the other room. And there were voices, but I couldn't tell whose they were.

I was just about to yell, "I'm home." Then I had a thought.

I put down my books and the mail. Quietly, I tiptoed across the kitchen toward the light coming from the living room and peeked around the doorway.

There were two candles burning, one on top of the TV and one in a pretty dangerous place—on the three-legged coffee table in front of the sofa. Ms. Henderson stood at one end of the sofa, her arms folded. A strange woman sat at the other end. I didn't see Matt anywhere.

I stayed in the shadow behind the door, holding my breath, watching, straining to hear. The woman was gathering some papers and stuffing them into a briefcase.

I saw her look down, as if looking at a watch. "She certainly should be home by now," she said.

Ms. Henderson didn't answer. Then, after a long time, she said, "Maybe she went to a friend's." There was this real cold sound in her voice. Was she mad? At me? For being late? Or was it something else?

"Does she do that often?" the woman asked.

Again Ms. Henderson didn't answer for a while. A lot of times she does that. It's like it takes a long time for words to get through to her. But I had the feeling that

*I stayed in the shadow behind the door, holding my breath,
watching, straining to hear.*

wasn't the reason she was silent now. I was almost sure she was mad. And the way she was standing there, not sitting, but standing, arms crossed, made me think that maybe it wasn't me she was mad at, but the person on the couch.

Eventually, after what seemed like a whole minute, she answered, "Often enough."

"Well, at least she's made friends here," the person said. She had a teacher voice, very important-sounding, the kind that makes everybody listen when she speaks. "That's a first for her."

A first! Huh! I had lots of friends other places—well, a few, anyway.

Ms. Henderson didn't bother to answer that at all.

A little part of me said, "Yay!"—as though she was sticking up for me by not answering. But I wasn't sure that was the reason for her silence at all.

I could see the person zip up the briefcase. "Well," she said. "At least if she's made friends, that says something for you, says something for the care you've given her. We'll take that into account when we make our decision."

Decision? What decision?

Ms. Henderson made some sound. But whatever it was, she didn't say it loud enough for me to understand her from where I stood.

But I could hear the other person clearly. "You have to understand," she said. "We just can't have our clients living in this kind of . . . of . . . "—she stood up and looked all around her—"situation," she said finally. You could tell that wasn't the word she meant.

"I'll be back," she went on. "We're still assessing this. It remains to be seen what . . . "

Something touched my leg. I jumped and barely

23

choked back a scream. As I stepped backwards, I put my foot on something—a small toy, a car—and I stumbled and almost fell as the thing squirted out from under my foot.

Immediately, the voices stopped.

"Is that you, sweetie?" Ms. Henderson's voice.

I didn't answer. I looked down.

It was Matt, tugging at the leg of my jeans. "We hate her," he whispered.

Then, like some weird joke, all the lights came on at once. And not just the lights, but everything. The TV blasted on, and the radio in my room came on, and behind me in the kitchen, I could hear the rumble of the refrigerator starting up.

The woman in the living room dropped her briefcase as if she'd been shot. She and Ms. Henderson turned, both of them blinking at the light. Both of them looking right at me, wide-eyed, as though I was the one who had done it.

Matt let go of my jeans leg. "TV!" he yelled. "The TV!" He raced past me into the living room and plopped down on the floor in front of it.

"Bailey," Ms. Henderson said.

"Bailey?" the woman said.

She wasn't any social worker I'd ever seen before, but I knew right away she was one. She was wearing a blue skirt and a white blouse, and her shoes were old-lady tie shoes. Her legs and ankles were straight and chunky like tree trunks. Even if it wasn't for her clothes and her shoes, you could tell she was a social worker because she looked like every other one I've ever had—sort of tired.

I didn't hesitate for even a second. I walked straight over to her. "Hello," I said, with my best grown-up manners. I gave her my dazzling, charming-fake smile that I'd learned from one of my foster moms. "I'm Bailey Wharton." And I held out my hand to shake hands. I was going to find out right now what was going on.

She just stood there staring at me as though she were in shock, maybe because of the sudden light and noise. Or maybe because she hadn't expected me to come shake hands and say hello like this. I didn't know what the other social workers had told her, but I could guess. Hah! I could be anything or any way I wanted to be. Depended on what I wanted. Right now I wanted information.

I kept my hand there in front of her. She just looked at me and then at my hand. Hadn't she ever shaken hands with a kid before?

After a minute, she seemed to recover, and she took my hand. Hers was dry and papery, but she smiled at me. "Nice to meet you, Bailey," she said. She didn't look quite as tired when she smiled. "I'm Miss Rothbart."

Miss Rothbart, who? I thought. I just waited.

"Your new social worker," she said, as if she had read my mind.

"You came to see how I was doing?" I asked.

She looked toward Ms. Henderson. "Not exactly," she said.

I leaned in a little closer. "Then you came for another reason?" I asked.

She seemed a little uncertain. She sat back down on the sofa. I sat down, too, and leaned forward toward her.

"Uh, how do you like it here?" she asked.

This part got tricky. I wasn't sure what to say because I wasn't sure what she wanted to hear. Did she want to know about me? Or about living with Ms. Henderson? From what I had overheard, I wondered if maybe it wasn't me she had come about at all.

"It's . . . okay," I said slowly, and wondered if that was the right thing to say. I slid a look at Ms. Henderson, but she wasn't looking back. Should I say it's great? That I loved living without electricity?

Though we sure had plenty now. Miss Rothbart practically had to shout over the TV, and she had pulled her shoulders up toward her ears as though she could shut out the noise. "Are you being treated all right?" she shouted.

I heard her perfectly well, but I said, "Pardon me?" Super-polite.

She leaned forward and shouted it again. "Are you being treated all right? How are your . . . living conditions?"

"Fine," I said. I didn't think I could go wrong with that answer. Then I added something because of what I'd heard before, something she seemed to think was important. "I have friends here," I said.

"That's very good," she said. She smiled, and again she seemed less tired-looking.

"*Lots* of friends," I said.

"That's . . . important."

I didn't really see why it was important, but if she thought so, I'd give her more of it. But first I turned to Matt. "Would you turn that thing down?"

He did—a little—and I felt I could breathe again.

I went on. "Yes," I said. "I'm even—"

I hesitated. I was going to say, "I'm even president of the fifth grade." But I was afraid she'd check. So I told the truth. "I'm even running for president of fifth grade," I said. Then I added, "I'll probably win. I have lots of people voting for me."

I didn't tell her what Kevin and I had been planning

26

all afternooon—finding ways of bribing people to vote for me. I didn't think that was any of her business.

"Well, my word!" she said. She looked from me to Ms. Henderson. "That does make a difference, doesn't it?" She pulled out her notebook and wrote something down.

"A difference?" I squinted at her and forgot to be charming. "What kind of difference?" I asked.

She didn't answer. She just stood up, after carefully putting her notebook in her briefcase. Then she slid her arms into her coat. "Well," she said, "this may be good news." She looked at Ms. Henderson, who was staring at the TV. "I'll be following how you're both doing."

Both? Then she left, and Ms. Henderson didn't walk her to the kitchen and to the door outside.

As soon as she was gone, I turned to Ms. Henderson. "What was that all about?" I asked.

Ms. Henderson only shook her head. Her look is always vague and kind of spacey, but this time it was even more so, as if she wasn't even inside her own face. I had no idea what she was thinking.

"It's only fair to tell me, you know," I said. Suddenly I was fighting back tears. "Was all of this just because of the electric bill?" I could barely keep the tears out of my voice. "Or . . . something else?" I couldn't say what I was wondering: *Is it because you want to get rid of me?*

Ms. Henderson blinked, as if she was just waking up. Then she looked at me and said the stupidest thing: "I never know what you're thinking."

"I never know what *you're* thinking!" I said.

We both just stared at each other.

She sighed. "Do you like living here?" she finally said.

27

"Do you want me living here?" I said back.

Matt looked up from the TV. "We want you here," he said. He looked at Ms. Henderson. "Right?"

She smiled at Matt, but she didn't answer. I suddenly had the funniest thought: *She's as stubborn as me.*

She turned back to me. "Are you really running for president of your class?" she asked quietly.

I nodded.

"You never told me."

"You never asked." I knew that was mean. It had started only today.

"I hope you win," she said. She made it sound so important, so urgent, that Matt looked up from the TV again.

"I really hope you win." And she went out of the room.

I just stood there staring at the door. Why had she said that? Because she knew, too, that the social worker might take me away—unless I could prove I had friends? Unless I could win the election?

If she wanted me to win, that meant she—maybe— *wanted* me, wanted to *keep* me? Didn't it? *She wanted to keep me!*

Suddenly I got scared. I wasn't sure that this was what I wanted. I mean, I wanted to stay here with my friends and all. I did. But did I want Ms. Henderson and Matt as my family? For good? Or for a long time, anyway? I'd never been with anybody longer than a year.

I looked at Matt, stretched out on the floor, humming "The Electric Company" closing song. He shook his hair out of his eyes and looked up at me. He said something in Spanish and then grinned at me.

I didn't answer. I just looked back at him. Was this really the family I always dreamed of getting?

Matt was trying to get me to answer him, saying something over and over in Spanish. But since I can't speak Spanish, the words didn't make any sense to me, not any more sense than the thoughts going round and round in my head.

4

THE NEXT MORNING and every morning for the rest of that week, Kevin and I met by the newsstand and rushed to school early—way before anyone else, even Miss Holt. We were working on my campaign for president. The first part of the campaign was our secret plan. The plan was to make a list—a list of each kid and one important thing each one wanted. Then we'd get it for them *if* they would vote for me. We knew it would cost money, maybe lots of it. But I get paid for baby-sitting Matt, so I always have some money, even though Kevin's always broke.

We hadn't told anybody else about our plan yet— not even Brant. And I hadn't told anyone, not even Kevin, how important it was that I win. Not just to show Janie and them. But because to Miss Rothbart, the social worker, it seemed to make the difference in whether or not I stayed here. Because I was beginning to think I really wanted to be here. Not that I wanted Ms. Henderson as my mother for good. I didn't. I'd thought about that a lot ever since Miss Rothbart showed up. I'd never had a mother that I knew of, and I wasn't looking for one now. But maybe I could stop moving around so much for a while. And since Ms. Henderson wanted me to win the election, maybe she was hinting that she wanted me to stay, too. The whole thing confused me. But I did know this: I had never had a friend like Kevin before, and for the first time in my life, I wasn't looking for a way to move on. I wanted to stay right here for a while.

On Friday of that week, Kevin and I had each finished our own lists and were going to compare them. At first, even though I was the one who'd thought up the plan, I got a little nervous about it. But not Kevin. He was real excited.

"It's like bribing people," I said. "You said it yourself that day. You can get in trouble for that."

"Nah," Kevin said. "In real campaigns they bribe people."

"Do not."

"Do too. They give out stuff like buttons and balloons and all. That's sort of bribery, right? And that's all we're doing."

I shrugged. "I guess."

"So," Kevin said. "Same thing. Only we give out other stuff."

He got out the notebook where he'd written "Bailey for President!" and took a piece of paper out of it. "Here," he said. "Here's my list."

I took out my list, too, and we exchanged them.

As soon as he got mine, he began shaking his head. "You think we can really buy votes this way?" He read from my list. "A kitten for Jennifer. . . . How you going to get a *kitten?*"

"I don't know. But the list isn't what we can do. It's only what people want. We'll figure out later what we can do. Just read."

He shrugged and went back to reading. I did, too.

His list was boring: Candy for Brant. Garbage Pail Kid cards for Craig. Snoopy pencils for Joe . . .

I handed the paper back to him. "Be creative!" I said.

"You call this creative?" He waved my list. "A horse for Sarah? How you going to get a horse for Sarah?"

"I'm not. But she wants one."

"Well, I want a scooter bike. Does that mean I'm going to get it?"

"You don't understand," I said. "We find out what people want. Then, if we can't get it, we still know something important. Like, think—Sarah wants a horse. Well, maybe we can't find a horse for her—"

"Maybe!" he interrupted.

I ignored him. "But we know that anything to do with a horse would work. A stuffed horse. Or a free horse ride somewhere. Or horse detergent to wash her horse once she gets one."

Kevin made a face, but I could tell he was thinking about it.

"Try it," I said again.

He picked up his pencil and the notebook. "Okay," he said, even though he still looked doubtful. "Brant. What's Brant really want?"

Right away we both laughed. Brant's in love with Miss Holt, and everybody knows it.

Kevin shrugged and wrote "Miss Holt" next to Brant's name.

"Owen," I said next. "He's easy."

"Yeah?"

"Yeah. You know how he can't write worth a poop?"

Kevin nodded.

"So we promise to write a report for him when the next one's due."

Kevin ran his tongue over his retainer and sucked on it. "A report? That's a lot of work."

I nodded. It was. I wasn't sure I wanted to work that hard either—not for just one vote.

"A letter?" I said. Miss Holt's really big on letter-writing these days—business letters, personal letters, all that.

Kevin grinned. "Perfect. Next homework assignment on letters—Owen gets one free."

"Right," I said.

"Right," Kevin said. He wrote it down in the note-book. "Jason?" he said next.

"Jason's a candy freak," I said.

Kevin nodded.

"A week's supply of Mike and Ike's," I said.

Kevin sighed. "Sounds expensive."

"So? It costs money to run for office."

"Yeah." He sounded kind of glum. Still, he wrote that down, too.

"Stephanie?" he said next.

"A diet," I said.

"You forgot your own rule," Kevin said. "What does she *want*?"

"Twinkies!" We both said it together.

He wrote it down. Then he said, "Donald?"

Donald. I rolled my eyes. Donald's even weirder than Owen. Well, not quite, because it would be hard to be that weird. But almost. Donald spits when he talks, and when he's not talking, he makes slurping sounds like he's trying to keep the spit back in his mouth. But it doesn't work. What did Donald need?

"A bib?" I said.

Kevin laughed so hard that his retainer flew out of his mouth and onto the desk.

"Gross!" I said.

"What's gross?" someone said.

I recognized that wimpy voice. Janie.

You! I thought. But I didn't say it out loud.

We looked up. It *was* Janie, standing by the coat closet, holding a backpack that was crammed so full that it looked like she had a watermelon in it. Knowing her, I figured she'd probably tiptoed in to spy on us.

"What are you doing?" she asked, looking straight at Kevin as though I wasn't even there.

"Working on Bailey's campaign," Kevin said. But he closed the notebook so she couldn't see.

I gave him a *look.* He tries to act so tough, but underneath he's really too nice. He can't even ignore a wimp like Janie.

"*Campaign?*" Janie said. She looked at me then and raised her eyebrows. She smiled, that better-than-you smile. I knew just what she was thinking: *Who'd vote for you?*

I looked her right in the eye and didn't let myself wonder about the answer to that question.

She went over to her desk and laid down her things real carefully, as though it wasn't a watermelon but a baby she had stuffed inside her backpack.

Kevin and I both watched her for a minute. She began taking a lot of stuff out of the bag. There was a huge stack of colored papers that looked like posters or ads or something. On the very top was a plastic bag filled with— candy?

I stretched to see better. It *was* candy—a clear plastic bag filled with Tootsie Roll Pops, each one tied with a little pink ribbon, each with a note attached. I couldn't see from my desk what the notes said, but I didn't have to see. I knew what they said: "Vote for Janie—Janie for President."

*Kevin laughed so hard that his retainer flew out of his mouth
and onto the desk.*

Talk about bribery!

But that did it. I wasn't at all worried anymore about what we were doing.

"What's all the stuff for?" Kevin asked her.

"Something."

Miss Holt came in the room then, carrying her thermos of coffee and her papers.

She smiled at all of us. "Working so early?" she said.

Janie smiled back. "Look, Miss Holt," she said. "This is the start of my campaign. My father helped me. And my mother. I have posters—lots and lots of them. We did them all on the computer last night. And they're even in color!"

I looked at Kevin.

He sighed.

Miss Holt said, "That's nice, Janie." She turned to me, still smiling. "And how's your campaign doing?"

I just shrugged.

How was I supposed to compete with a computer that made colored posters? Or lollipops with pink ribbons? I sighed. This was going to be harder than I had thought.

Miss Holt turned to the blackboard and began writing out the list of the things we'd be doing that day.

When she turned away, I made a face at Kevin.

"Don't worry," he said quietly.

But I could tell he was glum, too.

We looked up at the list on the board. Another boring day. Science reports. Letters—personal letters. Personal letters? Personal letters! And suddenly I had an idea!

I took a quick look at Janie to see if she was snooping. She was—looking right at Kevin and me. I took out my notebook and scribbled something. I poked Kevin. "Get a load of this!" I said.

Kevin read what I had written, then looked up at me. "You're going to write to *him*?" he said, right out loud.

I poked him again. "Shush up," I said, and I nodded toward Janie. Then I said quietly, "Yup."

"You're weird!"

"Am not," I said. "Think about it! He knows all about running for office—running for the presidency. I'll just write to him and ask him to write to the class and tell them to vote for me. I'll tell him what a great president I'd make and everything."

"He'll never do it."

"He might."

"Where would you get his address?"

"Don't have to. Just write to the White House—'The White House, Washington, D.C.' All the mailmen know where it is, I bet."

Kevin smiled. "Boy, and if he did answer, I'll bet everybody'd vote for you. Be just like getting a letter from God."

I nodded. "Yup. They'd be impressed right out of their skulls."

Kevin looked at the list we'd been working on before. "Think we can forget the rest of our plan?" he asked.

"No," I said. "I think we have to do both. Because I don't know how long it will take to get a letter back."

I looked over at Janie, who was dumping her lollipops out on the desk, lining them all up in rows. "And when I do get the letter," I said softly, "it won't matter if Janie has a trillion lollipops with solid gold ribbons."

38

President of the United States
The White House
Washington, D.C.

Dear Mr. President:

Miss Holt, my teacher, is making us write "personal letters." They're called friendly letters, and they're different from business letters. Personal letters have to go to someone who is important to us personally—like our grandparents, or if they're all dead, even our parents. I think that's pretty stupid. (Nobody else will see this letter—it's our rough draft, and the teacher doesn't read it.)

Anyway, we have to write to somebody important, so I picked you. I really don't have anyone like a parent or a grandparent, so I hope you don't mind.

I thought you should know why I picked you to write to. What made me think about you is that I want to do something you did once. I want to run for president—not of the United States, but of my class. It's really important that I win. And I knew you'd be the perfect one to help—being a president yourself and all that. So this is what I would like you to do: I would like it very much if you would write to my whole class, but send the letter directly to me. In the letter, tell the class that they should vote for me. If you tell them to, I know they will. And they'll be real impressed that I have someone as important as you for a friend.

Since I know so much about you from the papers and all, I think it's only fair that you know something about me. That way, in your letter that you're going to write, you'll be able to give the reasons why I'd be a good president.

I am eleven years old and in fifth grade at Burke School. I get pretty good grades when I feel like it. If I get to be class president, I'll probably feel like it a lot more often. I don't have many friends who are girls. Well, I don't have any. But I do have one friend who's a boy—not a boyfriend, just a friend who's a boy. His name is Kevin Corbett, and he's my best friend. It took him a while. I mean, I could tell he wanted to be friends, but he was scared to have a friend who's a girl! Isn't that stupid? Or are you that way, too? (I guess not, though. Presidents have to like girls, or else girls won't vote for you.) But he's gotten over it, and we're good friends now.

Anyway, I'm kind of skinny, and I have blond hair and greenish eyes, and I'm pretty short for my age. I hope someday I'll get to be tall because I think that's important for a woman. When I told that to Ms. Henderson, my new foster mom, she agreed. But I'm not sure she really meant it. Lots of times she says, "Yeah, sweetie," when she's not even listening.

She calls everybody "sweetie." The first day I was here, she said I could call her "Mom" if I wanted to. But I don't. She's not my mom. Jeez, if I did that with each of my foster moms, do you know how many moms I'd have? Eleven.

I forgot to tell you the reason I want to be president. It's because all the class presidents will be on the student council that will help run the school. Of course, grown-ups don't really let kids run anything. So there's another reason, but I don't want you to say anything about it in the letter you write back. You know how I told you that I don't have many friends who are girls—well, really any friends? That's because Janie leads the pack of girls and Janie doesn't like me, so they don't, either. Not that I care that much. But if I got elected president, that would show them that I was pretty important, that people do want me. But even more than that—I might have to get moved from here if I don't win. It's a little hard to explain why, so you'll just have to believe me that it's true.

Janie's running for president, too. She's sitting over there now, twisting her hair around and around her finger and then chewing on the string of twisted hair. She always does that when she's concentrating. That's because she's trying so hard to find something terrific to say—probably to her own mother! And she just saw her mother this morning.

I read the other day that some doctors operated on this lady and took a four-and-a-half-pound hairball out of the lady's stomach. That's because she used to chew on her hair all the time. Do you think the same thing could happen to Janie? I keep looking to see if she's getting fatter in her stomach where the hairball would be growing. But she's not.

Miss Holt just said that we're going to make a bulletin board with the letters we receive back. So please write back! Janie will probably get the first letter back—from her own mother!

When I heard about the bulletin board, I thought maybe I'd write to my foster mom and ask her to write back. But she doesn't write real well, and the kids might make fun of the letter. And the only thing she reads is this newspaper that has all the weird stories in it—like about the hairball.

I hope you'll write back to me. I collect the stamps when anyone writes to me. So if you wrote back, I'd put the stamp from your letter in a special place in my stamp book.

Well, I got to go now. Just remember to write and tell the class that I'd be a great president, and tell them the reasons why. And then tell them that they should vote for me. Don't be too fancy or anything. Just a regular letter. And maybe some-

day when I'm older I can do something for you. Like vote for you or something.

  Please, please, please answer real quick.

                                    Yours respectfully,

                                    Bailey Natalia Wharton
                                    Grade Five

  P.S. Janie's still sucking on her hair. If she doesn't get her letter done pretty soon, her hairball will be up to five pounds, I bet.

6

WE'D BEEN WRITING and revising letters for a week. And working on our campaigns for president for a week. The one good thing that happened was that we were down to just three candidates for president—Janie, me, and Donald. Lots of people were dropping out just because nobody wanted to have to give a campaign speech. And Donald was no threat at all. The only one who would vote for him—besides himself—would be Owen. So the rest of the votes would be divided between Janie and me. Although, if we believed Janie, the votes wouldn't be divided at all. She bragged that she had practically all the girls' votes.

She probably did, too, since she was bribing them with lollipops, but also with other sneaky stuff. Practically every other day she had a different—and best—friend. Whenever I saw her in the hall, she had her arm linked through someone else's. She made me want to throw up.

But even if Kevin and I could get all the rest of the boys besides Donald and Owen, I'd still lose unless we could change some minds.

Kevin and I were working hard on it. We were

promising lots of stuff to lots of people, and it was beginning to be lots of work. And expensive.

The big problem, though, was that I still hadn't gotten a letter from the President. Everybody was waiting for answers to the letters we'd sent out, but nobody wanted one as much as I did. I had already made a bet with Kevin about who'd have the first letter. Kevin said Owen. I said Janie.

At the end of the week, Miss Holt said that Kevin and I could put up the bulletin board for the replies, and we were going to be allowed to decorate it. On the day we were going to do the bulletin board, I met Kevin by the corner newsstand, and we rushed to school super, super early. But Miss Holt was there before us. Sometimes I think she sleeps at school.

We had decided to decorate the bulletin board with stamps. We'd put stamps from different places in the world all around the edges of the board. Since I write so many letters and collect so many, I have lots of different kinds of stamps. And everywhere I've lived, I've collected all the stamps that came on letters. I have about three thousand stamps now.

Kevin and I were just starting to put up the board when Janie arrived.

"I got a letter back, Miss Holt," she yelled. "I got one!" She had an envelope in her hand, and she waved it over her head as though she were playing Capture the Flag. "From my grandmother."

I looked at Kevin. "Told you," I said.

Kevin made a face. "She probably wrote it to herself." He said it quietly, but like always, Janie heard. It's as if she's got elephant ears.

"Did not!" Janie said. "My grandmother wrote it. And my mother said that must have been very hard for her to do because my grandfather died last year and she's still very sad."

"Big deal," I said.

"And you know what else?" Janie said. "It came all the way from Italy! Express mail!"

"Big deal," I said again.

Miss Holt frowned at me, then smiled at Janie. "How nice, Janie," she said.

I rolled my eyes. "We should send Janie express mail to Italy," I said to Kevin. "In *two* boxes." I didn't say it loud enough for Miss Holt to hear, just loud enough for Elephant Ears. She made a face at me.

"What does the letter say?" Miss Holt said.

"I don't know," Janie said. "I can't read it."

"Can't read it!" Kevin and I both said it at the same time.

Even Miss Holt's eyebrows went up.

"Well, I can't!" Janie said. "Because it's in I—talian." That's just the way she said it, like two words: *I* and *Talian.*

"How nice!" Miss Holt said.

I think those are Miss Holt's safety words: "How nice!" She uses them a lot.

"I think it's pretty dumb," I said. "Why does she write in Italian if you can't read it?"

"Because she wants me to learn. To preserve my heritage, she says."

"What's that mean?" Kevin said.

Janie just shrugged.

She turned back to Miss Holt. "My father usually reads her letters to me, but he's away on a business trip. So I brought it in anyway."

"How nice, Janie," Miss Holt said again. "Why don't you put it up on the board now?"

Miss Holt got up then and started to go out in the hall to talk to the other fifth-grade teacher. She turned and smiled at Janie. "You'll have the first letter up there."

As if Janie needed to be told.

Janie came over to where Kevin and I were working. She sort of elbowed us aside, working her way in between us—and just the other day she'd been acting like she couldn't be near me because I smelled! Then she took four tacks and stuck her letter right in the middle of the board. Right in the very middle. Then she crumpled up the envelope and started to throw it away.

"Wait a minute!" I said. The stamp was really pretty. Even without looking at it too closely, I could see that it was unusual. It would be great in my collection. "Can I have that?"

Janie backed away from me a little. She smoothed out the envelope and looked at it. "Why?" she said, real suspiciously.

I just looked at her. Knowing her, I knew she'd keep it if I told her why. "No reason," I said.

"Well, if there's a *good* reason you can have it," she said.

I debated whether or not to tell her. Kevin looked at me and shrugged.

"Because I want the stamp," I said. I tried to sound real casual. "It's not a terrific one, but I collect stamps."

Janie looked down at the envelope in her hand. "Oh," she said. "I forgot. I collect stamps, too."

And she turned and took the envelope with her to her desk.

Kevin glared at her back. "We should stuff her in a cubby," he muttered.

I was too mad to even answer. But it was nice of Kevin to be mad for me.

We worked side by side for a while, putting more stamps around the edges of the board.

"I'm going to get her," I said. "I don't know how, but I will." I wanted to punch her out, but I knew I'd get sent to the office for it. I didn't feel like spending my morning listening to a lecture.

A lot of kids had begun to arrive. As they came in, they all clumped up around Kevin and me and the bulletin board, trying to see what we were doing. When Violet and Stephanie got there, Janie jumped up to stand beside her precious letter and show it off. Then Violet and Stephanie asked the same question that everybody else had been asking: "What does that say?"

That's when I got my idea.

I looked around. Miss Holt was still out in the hall.

"It's a very sad letter," I said.

"How do you know?" Janie said.

"I can read Italian," I said. I said it the same way she'd said it before—*I* and *Talian*—like two separate words. But she didn't even seem to notice I was making fun of her.

Of course I couldn't really read Italian, but Janie didn't know that.

"You didn't say so before," Janie said.

"You didn't ask me."

"So, what does it say?" Janie said.

I shook my head real sadly. "I don't think you want to know," I said.

Janie turned to Violet and Stephanie and made a face. "She's such a bragger," she said. She turned back to me. "You're just saying that because you can't read it. You're a liar."

I sighed. "Okay," I said. "But remember, you insisted. I didn't want to do it."

47

I turned my back to them and faced the bulletin board. I began pretending to read it, real slowly, as though I was trying to figure out the words.

"Dear Janie," I pretended to read. "I know that this will be a very sad letter for you to read. I had a lot of trouble and I am very sick. In fact, I'm probably dead by now. By the time you read this letter. I hope you have a good time for the rest of your life. I hope that you will be happy. Even if you don't get to be class president. Be good. Love, Grandma."

"That's not true!" Janie said. "You're lying."

I just shrugged.

I turned around. Violet and Stephanie had their hands over their mouths. Even Kevin looked horrified, as if he believed it. When I looked at Janie, there were big, fat tears in her eyes. As I watched, one tear rolled fast down her cheek, and then another one followed super fast.

Oh, hell.

I didn't mean to make her cry.

"It was just a joke," I said. "It's not true."

Janie began crying then. I mean, really crying, her shoulders shaking and everything.

"I was just joking!" I said. "It's not true!"

"That's *mean*!" Janie sobbed.

"I *know*," I said. "I'm sorry!"

But Janie had stopped listening to me. At first she'd just been plain crying. But then Violet and Stephanie each took one of Janie's hands and tried calming her down. As soon as Janie saw how much attention she was getting, then she really started—yowling and wailing and everything. She sounded just like Mrs. Hughes's cats when they wanted to get outside and mate.

Miss Holt appeared in the doorway. "*What* is all this

noise about?" she said. She took one look at us and hurried over. "Janie!" she said. "What is it? What's wrong?"

Of course Violet and Stephanie had to rush and tell her all about it.

"It was just a joke," I said. And Kevin and I went back to working on the bulletin board, trying to pretend that nothing had happened.

After Violet and Stephanie finished their story, Miss Holt was quiet for a moment. Then she said, "Bailey!"

I pretended not to hear. It works sometimes. The person who speaks to you waits for a minute or two, and then just gives up and goes away.

But not this time.

Miss Holt put a hand on my shoulder, then beckoned to me to follow her out into the hall.

Behind me, Janie began moaning and sniffling again.

Out in the hall, Miss Holt looked very mad. I've never seen her look quite like that, not even the day I pretended to be sick and went to the nurse's office six different times.

"That was very wrong of you," she said.

"I was just joking," I said. "And besides, she started it. And I did say I was sorry."

"I don't care who started it. There can be no excuse for that kind of behavior," Miss Holt said. She was looking at me so hard that her eyes were all squinted up. "Can there?" she added.

I started to say, "Yes, there can." But something about the way she looked stopped me. So instead I just said it to myself.

Both of us were quiet for a while.

After a minute, Miss Holt said, very softly, "Other people have feelings, too, you know."

I never said they didn't. But again I only said it to myself.

Miss Holt sighed.

Just then, Violet, Stephanie, and Janie appeared in the hall. Violet and Stephanie were on either side of Janie, holding on to her as if she were a very old lady who was going to drop dead in her tracks any minute.

"We're taking Janie to the lavatory," Violet said.

Janie didn't look like she needed someone to hold her up. But even I had to admit that she looked pretty awful.

"No," Miss Holt said, as if she had just made up her mind about something. "Stephanie and Violet, you go back in the classroom now. I think Janie should go down to the nurse's office and lie down for a while." She looked at Janie. "Would you like to do that?"

Janie nodded and snuffled some more. She reminded me of Owen, the fuzzy seal. Janie and Owen really should get married. They'd make a great pair. They'd probably have a real seal for a baby.

Miss Holt turned to me. She gave me a look as though warning me about something, but when she spoke, all she said was, "Bailey, will you please walk Janie to the nurse's office?"

I knew I didn't dare argue. But I let out a big, noisy sigh, just to let Miss Holt know how unfair I thought it was.

Neither Janie nor me spoke all the way downstairs. I knew just what Janie was thinking the whole time—she'd gotten all this sympathy from everybody and now she'd get lots of votes.

When we got to the bottom of the steps near the cafeteria, we could smell lunch cooking. It smelled like barbecued beef on a bun. It's really gross. Everybody calls it barbecued barf on a bun. But my stomach started grumbling, and I suddenly realized how hungry I was. Breakfast that morning had been half a can of Diet Slice and some Twinkies that I bought on my way to school. Ms. Henderson says I should eat cereal in the morning, but I don't, and she doesn't make me. She'd have to force-feed me the stuff she has, anyway. She buys only one cereal— a health cereal, she says. I bet those straw doormats they have outside the hardware store taste better than that cereal.

Across from the cafeteria was the nurse's office. But the nurse's door was closed, and there was a sign on it that said: THE NURSE WILL BE BACK IN A MINUTE. PLEASE HAVE A SEAT. There was a desk chair in the hall, right next to the door.

Janie looked disappointed. I could tell that she'd been hoping to get in there and have somebody else feel sorry for her. I should have told her that the school nurse doesn't get to vote in class elections.

I stood on my tiptoes and tried to peek through the window to see if the nurse, Miss Puckey, was in there, hiding out. She does that. I know because on the day I came down six times, four of those times the same sign was on the door. And three of the times I could see her at her desk, drinking coffee. I think that's pretty mean when a kid needs you to get out of class. But I guess I'd do the same thing, too, if I had to spend my whole day sticking thermometers in kids' mouths. This time, though, she really wasn't there.

Janie sniffed. "Smells like a hospital here," she said. She turned around and wrinkled her nose. "And the cafeteria smells worse."

I didn't answer.

"You going to buy lunch today?" Janie said.

Of course I was going to buy today. I had to. But it wasn't any of her business, and I didn't feel like talking to her anyway. I wondered why she was suddenly so friendly.

"How come you buy every day?" Janie asked. "Even on the gross days?"

I just shrugged.

"You're on free lunch, aren't you?" she said. "I bet that's why."

I glared at her. "I buy," I said, "because school lunches are nutritious." The exact same thing I'd said in the other schools I'd been in, the thing I'd practiced. I did get free lunch, but that's nobody's business. Certainly not Janie's.

She gave me her know-it-all look. "I bet," she said. Then she smiled. "Do you think anybody in class will really vote for you? Vote for somebody who's on *welfare*?"

"Think they'd vote for *you*?" I said. I wasn't going to talk to her about whether or not I was on welfare. That wasn't her business.

"My father says that people on welfare are all lazy," she said. "The only thing they're good at is using tricks to get out of working. He says if they weren't lazy, they wouldn't be on welfare. So how can somebody lazy be president?"

Her father must have been as stupid as she was. But I didn't know how to answer.

Not that she noticed. She went right on. "You might get one or two votes," she said. "But only from people who want to be on Kevin's good side. Nobody wants *you*."

And then I knew just what to do—what I'd been wanting to do ever since the day she gave that boring, boring, boring talk about the time pilot.

I turned my face away from her for a minute to get ready. I opened my mouth real wide, twisted up my tongue, and rolled my eyes back in my head. I couldn't see too well that way, but I reached out till I felt her, and I poked.

"Stop it!" she said. So I knew she was looking at me.

I turned around with my face all twisted up like that. And exploded my monster sound right into her face.

She screamed at the top of her lungs. And then burst into tears again and collapsed in the chair. "I'm going to tell!" she shouted.

I turned and started running up the stairs.

Behind me, I could still hear her yelling, "I'm going to tell! *Everything*. And nobody will vote for you! Nobody at all!"

I laughed.

Kids would vote for me. Already Kevin and I had four appointments after school that day. Kids were dying to sign up. But I was just a little worried, too. What if Janie told them what her father said—that I'd be too lazy to be a good president? I knew that was stupid. But would everybody else know that?

Yeah. They'd know. I'd prove it. No matter what Janie said.

7

AFTER SCHOOL THAT DAY, Kevin and I spent a long time with Jason, Jonah, Robby, and Craig. Jason and Jonah and Craig were pigs. They wanted Heath bars, Double Bubble bubble gum, and Mike and Ike's. Every day for a week.

Good thing Ms. Henderson paid me for baby-sitting. Still, that much gum and candy would take my whole week's supply of money. And on just three kids!

"No way!" I said.

Jason shrugged.

Jonah and Craig did, too, as though they weren't going to change their minds.

"It's what we want," Craig said.

"Can't!" I said. I folded my arms, stared at them, and waited.

Kevin poked me, but I ignored him. I knew he was afraid we'd lose their votes. But you've got to make bargains. I learned that long ago.

I just stood there, staring and waiting. I had a feeling they'd give in somehow.

After a minute of staring, Jonah leaned toward Jason, and they whispered together. Craig bent his head in with them.

"Okay," Jason said finally. "We'll cut out the gum."

I looked at Kevin. He nodded. But he'd nod at anything.

I knew I'd agree, too, but I pretended to be thinking about it. I made them wait for a long minute, and then I sighed and said, "Okay. But you've got to sign."

Kevin and I had figured it would be good to get all the deals in writing.

All of them bent over the campaign notebook that Kevin was holding. Kevin wrote down the deal, and the three of them signed.

When we got to Robby, he said, "You've got to collect my paper route."

Together, Kevin and I said, "Forget it!"

Robby grinned. I don't think he'd really thought we'd do it because right away he said, "Then deliver my Sunday papers."

Kevin groaned. *"Sunday?* Like in the *morning?"*

But I just shrugged. It meant getting up real early on Sunday. I didn't mind that much. Ms. Henderson makes me go to church, and I have to get up early anyway.

"Okay," I said. I didn't even feel like trying to bargain for something else. Besides, it was getting late, and I had to get home. So Kevin and I agreed, and we got Robby signed up, too.

We now had four sure votes besides our own. And Brant's made seven. Brant said he didn't know what he wanted, but I was pretty sure he'd vote for me even if he didn't get anything. We hadn't gotten to any of the hard ones yet—like Sarah and the horse or Jennifer and her kitten. But we'd figure something out. I knew it.

Kevin and I left each other at the corner, promising to meet next morning early. And to come up with some new ideas overnight, especially about Owen and Donald.

If we could get Donald not to run, we'd get his vote and Owen's, too. We'd have to think up something good.

When I got home, I could see Ms. Henderson at the door, waiting for me. Even though it was almost winter, the old, broken screen door was still up, and she had pushed it open, as if she were trying to see out better.

"I'm here!" I yelled. "You can go!"

I rode my bike into the yard, parked it under the steps, and locked it up. Then I raced to the street and quick checked the mailbox. No letter from the President, no mail at all. Maybe Ms. Henderson had already picked up the mail.

I raced up the stairs, using my lucky way of coming in. I wondered if she'd be mad about me being late. But I didn't think so. That's one good thing about Ms. Henderson—she never gets mad or punishes.

Funny, though. When I was little, I used to feel jealous sometimes when kids said they were being punished. I even used to pretend sometimes that my foster parents had punished me when they hadn't. Because it seemed that it'd be nice to have someone worry if I was late. But since I've gotten big, I realize how stupid that is.

Ms. Henderson was out on the landing by the time I got there, her coat on, and hat on, too—that funny hat she always wears. It's fluffy brown fur and huge, so she looks as if she's wearing a whole rabbit on her head.

"Sorry I'm late," I said.

She nodded and gave me that vague smile she uses a lot. "Matt's watching 'The Electric Company,' " she said.

"Okay."

"And there's macaroni and cheese."

"Frozen?" I asked.

"Box," she said. She sounded kind of apologetic.

I shrugged. "S'okay."

I love macaroni and cheese, but the frozen kind is best. Ms. Henderson doesn't buy the frozen much, though, because it's expensive, she says. Instead she buys the kind that comes in boxes, with the cheese in little paper envelopes inside.

"You know how to fix it," she said. It wasn't a question. Matt and me practically live on macaroni and cheese. I've probably made it a thousand times since I've been here.

"Yeah."

She opened her mouth like she was about to say something, but instead she just looked at me for a moment—that is, I think she was looking at me. Her eyes don't focus real good, or at least, one of them doesn't. One looks right at you, while the other one looks over your shoulder somewhere. When I first came here, I kept turning around to see who she was looking at.

After a minute, she said, "Do you . . . like living here?"

As soon as the words were said, I knew what was about to happen. I could feel the tight, empty feeling come in my chest, as though my heart had stopped or gone away somewhere. I'd heard that question before—or one so much like it—in other houses that I knew. And again here, just a few weeks ago, when the social worker came.

"I mean," she said. "I mean, we're not—stuck with each other or anything. If we don't like it. If it's not working out . . . "

Inside of me, a voice whispered: *But I do like it. I like it here. It's the best place I've been in a long while. Janie and those girls stink, but I'm running for president. And I have a friend, Kevin. And I was beginning to hope you wanted me here. But you don't, do you?*

But I couldn't say it out loud because I knew what she really meant, what she was really trying to say: the same thing the others meant when they started talking like this. It meant they were going to get rid of me and were looking for a way out. If I told her the truth, told her how much I liked it, she'd feel sorry for me when she sent me away. And I didn't need that—not from her or anyone else.

So, tell her: *No. No, I don't like it here.*

But I couldn't say that, either.

I looked at her. It had gotten almost completely dark, and I couldn't tell whether she was avoiding my eyes or not. Maybe she was looking right at me with those freaky eyes.

I took a big, deep breath. It started to come out quivery, so I stopped it short. "S'okay," I said. "I like it okay." It was the best I could manage.

I didn't wait to see how she reacted. "I'll go watch TV with Matt," I said, and I started into the house.

"Bailey!"

I turned around, surprised. She'd never called me by my name before. She always just calls me "sweetie," or else she waits till I'm looking at her before she speaks to me. I know all about that trick because that's what I used to do with all the foster parents who made me call them "Mom" or "Dad."

"I'll go to the store tomorrow," she said. "For frozen macaroni and cheese." And she turned and went down the steps.

I bet she'd forget.

I went into the house.

I knew why she said she'd get frozen macaroni and cheese, the kind I like. I said it out loud: "Because she's going to dump me, and she's feeling guilty."

Rats.

Now what to do? Nobody ever got rid of me. I always left them first. As soon as I saw it coming, I did it first. I remembered what happened with that social worker a long, long time ago and what she said. I was about four years old, just about Matt's age, and she probably thought I was too little to understand. I'd been living with some people who didn't want me anymore, and the social worker was trying to find somebody else to take me. But nobody would. It was late at night, and we were in her office, and she was on the phone. I can still hear her voice because it was the first time I'd heard a grown-up cry. She said something into the phone about me not being such a bad little kid.

"But nobody wants her," she said. "So, at least for tonight, I'm going to have to take her home with me." And she did.

It was then that I decided I'd never, ever again live with anybody who didn't want me. I hadn't, either. As soon as I saw they didn't want me, I left. Fast.

"Hey, Matt!" I yelled.

Matt was sprawled on his stomach on the living room floor in front of the TV. One of the couch pillows was balanced across the back of his head.

He dumped the pillow off and turned over when I came in. Then he grabbed the pillow again and pulled it tight over his face.

"S'dark under here," he said.

"Yeah," I said. "Usually is when you put stuff over your face."

"S'darker as night," he said.

"Right," I said.

He sat up and shook his hair out of his eyes. He has thick, soft, reddish hair. It's kind of long and just flops all around his face. He held out the pillow to me. "You do it," he said.

"No, thanks," I said. "You hungry?"

"Yeah." He jumped up and threw the pillow into a corner.

"Come on," I said. "Macaroni and cheese."

Together we went to the kitchen. We've done this so many times, we know just what to do. I always do the stove part because Matt's too little. So while I put the water on to boil, Matt tugged a chair over to the refrigerator and climbed up to get out the milk and margarine.

The whole time he was doing it, he was counting out loud in Spanish. He's been learning Spanish on "The Electric Company," and he loves it. He even makes his mom read him all the Spanish signs on the buses and stuff. He's really super-smart for four years old.

"Matt?" I said.

He stopped counting.

"Does Ms. Hen—does your mom—?"

"What?" Matt said.

"Nothing. But uh, do *you* like me being here?"

"I like it," he said. "You cook good."

But does *she* like me being here? I couldn't ask it.

"Mom says you cook good, too," Matt said.

"Yeah?"

"Yeah." He went back to counting again.

So, that's important, isn't it? She needs me to cook for Matt when she goes to work. So maybe she's not trying to get rid of me. Maybe what she said before about us not being stuck with each other was just talk—maybe she'd just been thinking about the social worker or something. Maybe she said she'd get something I like because she just wants to do something for me.

While I put the water on to boil, Matt tugged a chair over to the refrigerator and climbed up to get out the milk and margarine.

"Come on, Matt," I said, after a minute. "Macaroni's done."

Matt came over to me, walking very slowly and carefully, carrying the milk that he had already poured out into a measuring cup. He loves the next part—he gets to pour the milk and margarine and powdered cheese over the hot macaroni.

I picked him up so he could reach. He poured the stuff in and mixed it all around until the margarine melted and the whole thing turned a nice orangish color.

We divided it into two bowls and sat down at the kitchen table to eat. I was hungry. It was okay. She wasn't sending me away. She needed me to cook for Matt. To baby-sit Matt.

When we were finished, Matt said, "Read me a 'tory."

"Story," I corrected. "Sss. *Story.*"

Matt pushed out his lips, concentrating really hard, and said, " 'Tory!"

"*Story!*" I said. "Like this—sssstory!" We've done this about a million times. I don't know when he'll learn to pronounce his s's. For such a smart kid in Spanish, he sure has trouble with English.

"Ssss," Matt said. "Ssss, ssss, ssss. Ssss!" He slid down from his chair and crawled under the table. "Ssss!" He began nudging his head against my leg.

"What are you supposed to be?" I said.

"A 'nake!" Matt said.

"Snake!" I said. "Sss—nake!"

" 'Nake!" Matt said.

I gave up. "Go get a book," I said. "And I'll read your story. But first you gotta help with the dishes."

Matt insisted on staying a snake. So I washed the pots and plates and put them down on the floor in front of him, and he dried them down there, hissing the whole time.

Then he slithered off to his room and crawled back with his favorite book—*Serafina the Giraffe*. Since he was still a snake, he wouldn't get up on the couch. So we settled down together on the living room floor, with the pillow from the couch behind us.

Matt was still making his snake sounds. "Ssss," he said. "Sssss—tory. Sss—ocial worker!"

"*What!*" I said.

"Sss—stocial worker!" He grinned at me. "I said it! I said it—stocial!"

I took a deep breath. "Matt," I said, real casual. "What about social workers?"

"We don't like her," he said.

"Who?"

"The one today. And she 'tunk." He held his nose to show me. " 'Tinky!"

"Yeah?" I said, still trying to sound very calm. "Where'd you see her? What'd she want?"

"Here. In the living room." He opened the book. "Now read me."

I began reading, my mind racing. The social worker had come here. So what? No big deal. It's her job. That's what she's supposed to do—to see how I'm doing, how Ms. Henderson's doing. That's what social workers do.

But no, the social worker always came to see *me*, came when I was there. Unless there was something wrong, like last time with the electricity. Or unless Ms. Henderson had called her—told her to come, said there was a problem. Like the time with the Blounts when they called the social worker to take me away because they said I was stealing stuff. When I wasn't. When it was their own kid who was stealing.

I read, hardly thinking about the words. Why does Matt always pick the longest story when I have stuff on my mind? I knew I wouldn't be able to skip any parts either because Matt has it memorized. I was about halfway through, when I noticed that Matt was very still beside me. His head was resting against me, and his breathing was real quiet and regular.

"Matt?" I said softly.

I peeked down at his face.

His eyelashes rested on his cheeks. He was sound asleep.

Very quietly, I closed the book.

Immediately, Matt sat up. "You didn't finish!"

" 'Cause you were asleep."

"I wasn't!" he said. And he began to cry.

There was no sense arguing with him. Once he got tired like this, he was a big, cranky pain.

I finished the story, then helped him brush his teeth and wash and get into pajamas. Fortunately, he had forgotten about being a snake, so he didn't crawl into the bathroom. When he finally got into bed, I tucked him in the way he likes it—with the blankets so tight around him he can barely move. He calls it being tucked in "tight as a mouse." Not that I've ever heard of a mouse being tucked in like that.

When I was finished, I said, "Night, Matt," and closed the door real fast behind me.

This was the part I hated. I just knew what was coming.

"I'm not tight as a mouse!" he called through the door.

I knew it. Tonight wasn't going to be any different. "That's your fault," I called back. "I tucked. You wiggled."

65

"Pats," he said. He sounded kind of pitiful. He means he wants to have his face patted.

"I already *gave* you pats," I said. "A thousand of them. Now go to sleep."

He was quiet for a minute, and I took a deep breath and started to tiptoe away. But then I heard him call again. " 'Nuggles?" he said, real softly.

I sighed. Snuggles.

I went back and opened the door. "Okay," I said. "But just one."

He sat up and tossed all the covers aside, and now I'd have to tuck him in all over again. He was really very much a pain.

I sat down on the bed next to him, and he put his arms around my neck. I hugged him and he hugged me back, and we snuggled like that for a minute. He smelled sweet, like soap and just plain baby smell, even though he wasn't much of a baby anymore.

And I suddenly thought—*I'm going to miss him*. Not just Kevin. Not just running for president. I'm going to miss Matt. And even stupid Ms. Henderson!

I pulled away. "Go to sleep, Matt!" I said.

Matt slid down into his bed then, and I tucked him in again. Again I said good night. This time he let me close the door and go without yelling for anything more.

I stood outside his door for a moment. Even though I was always glad to get him to bed, I also wished sometimes that he was more grown up so he could stay up and talk to me. Especially tonight. Because now came the time of the day I hated most, when he was asleep and everything was quiet and there was nobody there but me.

After a minute, I went back in to the living room. I had to work on the plan for being president, even though I knew that maybe it was already too late to change things.

Still, if I won, there was just a chance—a chance to prove to Ms. Henderson and Miss Rothbart that I had friends, that I was worth keeping. But even if it was too late for that, it was more important than ever that I win. Because if I was going to have to leave here, I was going to leave as *somebody*: Bailey Natalia Wharton, president of the fifth grade.

I got out my notebook. But as I worked, I kept thinking about the social worker. Not the one from today, but the one from long ago. Because sometimes, at the craziest times, I could still hear her saying those words: "Nobody wants her."

8

FOR THE NEXT WEEK, Kevin and I spent practically every
second on my campaign. For now, I refused to think about
whether or not I'd have to leave. If I had to go, I'd go.
No big deal. I'd done it lots of times before. So I didn't
think about it. I didn't talk about it, either, not even to
Kevin. I couldn't tell anyone, not even him, what Ms.
Henderson had been hinting about. Sometimes, though,
it was hard not to think about it. But I've learned ways
to keep thoughts away—the TV is good, if you turn it up
really loud. And riding a bike is good, too, especially if
you ride it really fast down hills. Stuff like that.

It's harder, though, when the thoughts come at night.
Sometimes, especially when Ms. Henderson was still at
work and Matt was asleep, I'd get up and get Shakespeare, my stuffed bear. I keep him hidden in my suitcase under my bed. I don't know where I got him, but
I've had him for as long as I can remember. The social
workers say that nobody knows who my mother is—that
somebody found me in a bathroom in a McDonald's when
I was just a few hours old. But I think maybe my mother
left Shakespeare there with me. So when the thoughts
come, I take Shakespeare out and hold him for a while. I

always put him back before I go to sleep because he belongs in my suitcase. That's his home.

But thoughts like that didn't come too often. And in the daytime, I was so busy campaigning, I didn't have time to think. Kevin and Brant were both busy helping me, too. Sometimes Kevin even acted as though he wanted me to win more than I wanted it.

In school, Miss Holt said we'd have something called a run-off election. That sounded funny—as though you climbed up on something and then ran off it. But what it meant was that the three of us who were running for president would put our names on the blackboard. Everyone would vote for one of us. The person who got the least votes couldn't run for president anymore. There would be only two left, and they'd be the two who would run. Miss Holt said that was the way they did it in real presidential elections, so we'd do the same thing.

I could have saved Miss Holt a lot of trouble. I knew who would be the winners—Janie and me. Janie had all the girls. I had Kevin, Brant, and four more of the boys, plus my own vote. So that gave me at least seven. That left Donald—Kevin and I hadn't been able to talk him out of running—with the rest. I wasn't really worried about Donald.

Miss Holt waited until the end of the day for the run-off election. She handed out little slips of paper for us to put the names on. I wrote my own name very carefully in big letters—Bailey Natalia Wharton—and waited for Miss Holt to collect the votes.

It took her forever because she gives us so much time to do the most simple stuff. So while I was waiting, I took out this story that I had cut out of that weird newspaper that Ms. Henderson gets and looked at it again. I had brought it to show Kevin after school. It's about these two kids who were in a car accident. Their parents were killed, and they were, too. But the heart of one of the kids was still beating, even though her brain was dead. And the other one's heart was dead, but her brain was alive. So the doctors did an operation, a head transplant. They took the head and neck that was okay off the one dead kid and put it on the other kid whose heart was still beating. The paper never said whether or not the kid lived or died. Well, I guess the one whose head they didn't put back on was dead, but I mean the other one. But I don't know whether any of it was true or not because they didn't give anyone's name or where it happened or anything.

I finished rereading the story just as Miss Holt came to collect the votes. I stuck the newspaper clipping in my pocket and dropped my vote into the shoe box she held out.

We all watched as Miss Holt went back to her desk to count the votes. She put the papers into three piles— mine, Janie's, and Donald's. But as she began dividing them up, I quickly saw that all three piles were about equal.

I looked at Kevin and he looked at me.

He frowned.

I watched Miss Holt again, counting as she added to the smallest pile, Donald's pile—three, four, five—more. Or was that my pile?

Miss Holt kept on, adding little slips of paper to *each* of the three piles.

Everybody was very quiet. I know we were all watching Miss Holt and trying to count with her. Only we didn't know whose pile was whose.

"Well, class!" Miss Holt looked up. She smiled, in that super-bright way that teachers have when they think they have some big news. "It looks as though two people are tied."

A tie? Me and Donald tied? How gross! Just because he was a boy, that's why. I bet the boys voted for him just for that reason.

"Who, Miss Holt? Who?" Everybody was shouting. "Which two? Who lost?"

Everyone was standing up, calling out. All but me. And Janie. She looked as smug as if she was already president of the world.

Miss Holt turned to Donald. "I'm afraid, Donald, that you're no longer in the running." Then she added quickly, "But you didn't lose by much!"

Donald's face got real red, and he looked down at his desk.

For just a minute, I felt sorry for him. It stinks to find out that they don't want you.

But then I realized—me! If Donald was out, that meant Janie and me were tied!

"What's that mean, Miss Holt?" Violet yelled.

"Will we have another run-off?" somebody else called out.

Miss Holt put up her hands to quiet everyone. When things settled down, she said, "It's between Janie and Bailey. This is what happened: Janie got nine votes. Bailey got nine votes"—she smiled at me—"and Donald got eight votes."

Again she smiled—at Donald this time. "So it was very close, you see," she said to him.

I got nine votes! Nine! So that meant, not counting Kevin and Brant and me and the four votes we'd paid for, that *two* other people wanted me for president.

I wished I knew who they were.

I looked at Kevin. He grinned.

In my head, I did some quick arithmetic. There were twenty-six kids in the class. If I could get the eight votes that had gone to Donald—eight and nine were seventeen—that would leave Janie with only the nine she already had.

But Janie had been doing some arithmetic, too. Already, she was whispering to Donald. Then she turned around to Ryan and said something to him.

Kevin leaned over to me. "As soon as the bell rings, head for the bike stand," he said.

"Right." I knew why. Four of the boys—Greg, Tim, Ryan, and Anthony—ride their bikes to school together every day. They do everything else together, too. They're like quadruplets or something—they have the same kind of bikes, same kind of sneakers, same jackets. They all laugh at the same stupid jokes—their own. Everybody calls them the Copycats. They don't even mind. They call themselves that, too, as if they were a band or something. We'd find out if they'd voted for Donald. If they did, we'd get them signed up to vote for me. Because if we got one vote, we knew we'd get four. I just hoped it wouldn't cost too much.

As soon as we got dismissed, Kevin and I raced to the bike stand. Brant came, too. We got there at the same time as the Copycats.

"Who'd you vote for?" Kevin asked right away.

"Donald," they said. All four at once.

" 'Cause he's a boy," Ryan said. "Girls are weird." He bent over to unlock his bike, and I could see the top of his underwear. It was blue with a red elastic waist, like those Superman Wonderalls that Matt wears.

And he thought *girls* were weird!

"Well, now you got to vote for a girl," I said. "So how about voting for me?"

"Can't," he answered.

"We already promised," Greg said.

"Promised?" Kevin said. "Janie?"

All four of them nodded.

"What'd she bribe you with?" I said, real disgusted. How did she get to them so fast?

Ryan looked at Greg and Anthony and Tim.

"She's lending me something," Ryan said. "And I'm letting these guys see it, too."

"What?" I asked.

"VCR tape," Ryan said. *Death Hug of the Giant Squid.* I already saw it. This giant squid squeezes people, and they break apart. It's cool. There's blood all over."

"Yeah," Tim said.

"Yeah," Greg and Anthony said.

And then they all got on their bikes.

Death Hug of the Giant Squid. I'd seen that movie. There's one part where the squid squeezes somebody so hard that the person's head rolls right off.

And that's when I got the idea. Brilliant! It was going to be hard to pull it off, especially since I hadn't warned Kevin or Brant ahead of time. But I had to do it. Four votes were a lot of votes.

"That's not so terrific," I said. "Worse things than that happen in real life. It's happened to me."

"Oh, sure!" Greg said. "You met a ninety-foot squid!"

"Yeah," Anthony said. "In your bathtub."

I made a face at him. Then I made my voice very quiet and serious. "Something happened to me almost like in the movie," I said. I paused for a long moment. "Something really awful."

I looked right at all four of them. It's a trick I learned from being with social workers—you can get away with telling the most berserk story and people'll believe you—

as long as you look straight at them. So I looked right into their faces and said it again. "Something awful."

My look seemed to work. "What happened?" Ryan said, almost in a whisper.

"Well . . . " I said.

I hesitated, this time for real. I'd have to tell them about not having any parents. And if I did, they could guess that I was a foster kid. Not that I cared that much. But I've never actually told anyone in this school except Kevin—even though Janie seemed to know. If Janie knew, everybody else did, too, so it probably didn't matter that much.

I looked at each one of them, took a deep breath, and then said, "You know how I don't have any parents? I'm sort of an orphan?"

They all nodded.

I was right. They did know.

I put my hand in my pocket and found the clipping. I crumpled it some, on purpose, so it would look old and worn out. Then I took it out and looked at it, but I didn't let them see what it was. "Well," I said, "something really bad happened to me and my family. It's right here in the paper, it was so awful."

"You're really in the paper?" Greg said.

"Really," I said. "I always carry it around with me. It made big headlines. Everywhere."

"You were headlines?" Ryan said. "Let me see!" And he reached for the paper.

I stepped back away from him.

"Aw, come on," Ryan said.

"Come on," Greg and Tim chimed in.

I shook my head. "Make you a trade," I said.

"For what?" Ryan asked. But I could tell he already suspected.

"Votes." Then I added, "And if you promise not to tell anyone."

I didn't want the whole class talking about this. Just in case somebody found out it was a joke.

Anthony whispered to Greg. Greg passed it to Tim and Tim to Ryan. And then Ryan said, "Okay. We'll vote for you."

"And you won't tell?" I said. "Promise?"

"Promise." All four said it at once.

"Promise!" Kevin and Brant said.

Kevin and Brant?

I looked at them. Oh, man. I hadn't meant to trick *them*. But there was nothing I could do about it now. Everybody was watching me, waiting.

"Okay," I said. "See, there was this automobile accident. And my mother and father got killed. And my sister got killed. And . . . " I paused. And then I added, very slowly, "And I got killed, too."

I smoothed out the paper and held it out to them to read.

"See?" I said when they were all finished reading.

Tim looked up. "That's not true," he said. But he looked kind of sick.

"Is it true?" Brant said. He looked like he was going to faint.

"That's gross!" Anthony said.

"You were really dead?" Kevin said.

I nodded. But I didn't look at him. I just prayed he wouldn't be mad later when I told him the truth.

"How did it feel?" Ryan said.

I shrugged. "How do I know? I was dead."

"So you have your sister's brain?" Anthony said.

"No. My sister's heart."

"But then you have her body," Anthony said.

"Well," I said. "It's very confusing."

They were all staring at me, then looking down at the paper, then staring at me again. I could tell they were really impressed. But more than that, I now had four more votes. Those four, with the four I already had, plus Kevin and Brant and me, meant I was up to eleven votes. If I counted the two people who had voted for me today who I didn't know, that made thirteen. Almost enough to win. If I bought one more vote, I was set!

And then Brant did it. "Can we see your scar?" he said.

9

"YEAH!" THE COPYCATS all said it at the same time. "Let's see your scar!"

I'm going to get you, Brant, I thought.

"Can't!" I said immediately. I put my hand on the collar of my sweatshirt. I thought frantically. Something. Some excuse.

"Come on. Let's see!" Ryan said.

"Can't!" I said again. "It's . . . " It's what? I came up with an idea. I tried to look modest or embarrassed or something. "It's—it's too far down," I said.

Ryan and Anthony exchanged looks. "It's only your *neck!*" Ryan said. "It can't be *that* far down!"

I shook my head. "No," I said.

And then I remembered. There was a kid in one of the schools I'd gone to long ago who'd bought a fake scar at Halloween. I bet you could buy them in stores that sold tricks and stuff. Maybe I could find one in a store near here.

"Maybe tomorrow," I said. "When I'm wearing a different kind of shirt. One that buttons."

Anthony got as wide-eyed as Brant does sometimes. "Is that the reason you always wear a sweatshirt—to hide your scar?"

Thank you, Anthony, I thought. I nodded.

"Gross!" he said.

But now my mind was racing. I had work to do. I had to get a scar. And I had to tell Kevin and Brant the truth. "Gotta go," I said, and I got on my bike.

The Copycats were already on their bikes, and they got ready to leave. "Promise tomorrow?" Anthony called over his shoulder.

"Meet me here," I said. "And don't forget—you promised to vote for me."

As soon as they were gone, I turned to Kevin and Brant. I had to tell them, and I had to do it right away. The longer I waited, the worse it would get.

Kevin hadn't said anything for the longest time. I wondered if he already knew.

"Is it really that far down?" Brant said when the others had gone. "It must have hurt a lot to cut off your head and neck and everything."

I just looked at him. He was so dumb. But I felt kind of bad, too, for tricking him.

With the bottom of my sweatshirt, I rubbed the handlebars of my bike. It's a huge one, the old-fashioned kind with fat tires and no hand brakes, just plain old coaster brakes. I'd saved up my own baby-sitting money for it and bought it in the Goodwill store here. I polished the handlebars and didn't look at Kevin and Brant.

"I was only fooling," I said.

There was a minute when nobody said anything. And then Kevin burst out laughing. "I knew it!" he said. "I knew it."

I looked up and smiled at him.

"What do you mean, you were only fooling?" Brant said.

I just shrugged.

"You mean it's not true?" he said.

I shook my head. "Nope."

"Then—then where'd the story in the paper come from?"

"It happened to somebody. Or the paper said it did. But it didn't happen to me. And I don't think it's even true."

"Then you . . . " Brant kept looking, first at me, then at Kevin. Finally he just stuck his hands in his pockets and glared at both of us.

But Kevin was grinning. "I knew it," he said. "I couldn't say a word because I was trying so hard not to laugh."

"You did not know," Brant said to Kevin.

"Not at first," Kevin said. "But as soon as I read the paper, I knew. Now, what're we going to do about a scar?"

"Cut off your head," Brant muttered, still glaring at me. "You'll get a real one that way."

"It's you and your big mouth that's the problem," I said. I mimicked his words. " 'Can I see your scar?' "

"So? How'd I know?"

"We could make one," Kevin said. "But out of what?"

"Isn't there a place around here to buy one?" I said. "Like a store that sells tricks?"

"I have an idea," Brant said.

"Yeah?" I said. I hoped it would be a good one. Not only because I needed it, but because he'd feel better if we used his idea. I really hadn't meant to make him feel bad.

"Yeah," he said. "Gum. Bubble gum."

"Bubble gum?" I said.

"Yeah. Pink bubble gum in long strands, glued to your neck."

I looked at Kevin, and he grinned.

79

"Yeah!" We both said it at the same time.

"Let's go," I said. And all three of us hopped on our bikes and took off for the candy store.

When we got there, we raced inside, and each bought a package of gum. Right away we opened the packages and started chewing. Then we got back on our bikes and headed for Kevin's house. There's never anybody home there in the afternoon, so it would be a perfect place to work.

We sat on the porch and chewed till the gum was really soft, then pulled it out into long, thin strings. It didn't take much time for us to make some long enough to wind around my neck. Since I couldn't put it on myself, Kevin and Brant did it, pasting the gum to my neck down by my neckbone, just under the collar of my shirt. When it first went on, it just felt sticky. After it was on for a minute, it turned stiff and pinched my skin.

"Feels gross," I said.

"Yeah," Kevin said. "But you're getting four votes for it. Lean your head this way." He stuck some more gum to the left side of my neck.

"It itches, too," I said. I wiggled my shoulders.

"Hold still," Brant said. He was working on the back of my neck. "And hold your hair up."

I did. I began to feel like I was really in an operating room, having a new neck glued on. If the story was true and they really did switch heads on those kids, I felt sorry for the one who got the new neck and head. Well, maybe I felt sorry for the other one, too. Still, Kevin was right. It was four votes.

When Kevin and Brant were finished, I let my hair down. We all stood up, and Kevin and Brant backed a few steps away across the porch to see how it looked. I stood there, holding my sweatshirt down away from my neck so they could see better.

They looked at me for a long time. They looked at each other, then back at me.

"So?" I said. "How's it look?"

They sighed, then both said it at the same time: "Like bubble gum."

Rats. I went in the house, and to the bathroom, and looked in the mirror. They were right. It looked just like bubble gum. And besides, when I'd been walking inside to the bathroom, the sweatshirt rode up over the fake scar. When I pulled the shirt back down, it stuck to the gum, and the gum got fuzzies all over it. Who'd believe in a fuzzy scar?

I went back outside, pulling my scar off as I went. "This is depressing," I said.

Kevin and Brant weren't on the porch when I came out. But just then they burst through the door behind me.

"Here!" Kevin shouted.

He held something out to me—a little plastic egg. Immediately I recognized it. Silly Putty! Of course. Why hadn't I thought of that? Silly Putty is a sort of gluey, stretchy kind of plastic—a lot like gum—that you can pull into any shape you want. But the best part about it is that it's flesh-colored. And it sticks and gets stiff if you leave it out of its egg for any length of time. We could make a scar that would really stay for the whole day.

"Perfect!" I said.

"*I* thought of it," Brant said.

I smiled at him. "Good," I said.

"Let's do it," Kevin said.

So, for the second time that afternoon, I sat on the

steps, and for the second time they began operating on me. It went a little easier this time, I guess because they'd done it before. And I guess because I could sit still better. Silly Putty wasn't as itchy as gum when it went on.

When they were all finished, we all raced into the bathroom together to look in the mirror. I wanted to see for myself how it looked.

It. Looked. Perfect. A thickish kind of flesh-colored scar, a lumpish line all around my neck.

We all grinned at each other in the mirror. I admired myself and my neck. It was really a neat-looking mess. I rolled my head, experimenting, trying to see what it would feel like to have somebody else's head and neck glued on.

"Four votes!" Kevin said.

"Four votes," I said. "And it didn't cost us a single thing."

"We ought to charge to see it," Brant said.

Hmm. I hadn't thought of that. But then I said, "Nah. I don't want to make a big deal of it. They might tell somebody, and then everyone will want to see it."

Kevin nodded. "And we'd better meet here early in the morning," he said. "To put it back on."

I nodded. Together, we began peeling off the scar, then rolled up the Silly Putty and put it back in the egg.

Tomorrow. All I had to do was get through tomorrow. We'd nail down four more votes for sure. Then if we could just somehow get one more vote, I'd be set.

And then, on to the elections. I'd show them, all of them, especially Janie and the other snooty girls.

Then it was funny how it happened. Maybe it was just in my imagination, just a fantasy. But I felt that I wasn't saying it just to Janie anymore. I was saying it to her, to the social worker, the one from long ago, the one who said, "Nobody wants her." *I'll show you,* I was saying. *You were wrong. Somebody does want me. Maybe not to keep. But they want me.*

10

I RACED TO KEVIN's house early the next morning so we'd have plenty of time to get the scar glued on. I had hardly slept all night, just thinking about the elections. And the scar. Could I get away with this? But I bet I could.

Brant got to Kevin's at the same time as I did, and once again, they glued the Silly Putty scar to my neck. I wore a shirt that opened at the neck, the one I wear for church, so I could show the scar and then cover it up again. When we were finished, I wiggled my neck around to see if the scar was loose enough that I wouldn't feel like I was choking all day. It felt okay.

"How's it look?" I asked.

"Awful," Kevin said. "Like somebody cut off your head and sewed it back on again."

"Professional," Brant said. "Maybe I should be a doctor someday." He grinned. "Think Miss Holt would marry me then?"

"That's all you think about," Kevin answered.

We all rode our bikes to school then. I went a little more slowly, being careful not to twist my neck around too much. I left my jacket partway open, so it wouldn't bunch up over my shirt and wrinkle my scar.

When we got to school, the Copycats were at the bike stand, waiting for us.

"She's wearing a button shirt," Ryan said as soon as he saw me.

"You gonna let us see?" Anthony said.

"Yeah, you gonna?" Greg and Tim said.

"Maybe," I said.

Kevin said, "Take your time, huh?"

"Did you see it already?" Ryan asked.

Kevin looked at me.

"Yes," I said.

"You, too, Brant?" Ryan said.

"Yes," I said again, before Brant could answer either. I didn't want to listen to Brant and Kevin pretending to be horrified or whatever at their first sight of my scar.

"Let's see!" Anthony said. And they all gathered around.

I took a deep breath, praying that I wouldn't laugh and that Brant and Kevin wouldn't, either. Slowly, I unzipped my jacket the rest of the way. It was hard to keep a straight face, but I realized nobody was looking at my face anyway, only at my neck. Carefully then, I unbuttoned my collar.

They all bent in close.

For a minute, nobody said anything.

Then Ryan said, "Awesome!"

"Gross!" Anthony said.

Greg and Tim were silent, just staring.

I looked over their heads at Kevin and Brant. Kevin's face had gotten all red, as if he was suffocating from trying so hard not to laugh. But Brant was staring at my neck like he was fascinated by the scar.

I thought I'd burst trying not to laugh. I could feel

my face and neck getting red with the effort. Then I thought: *My scar! My neck will be red, and my scar won't.*

I put my hand up to cover it.

Anthony's face was practically on my neck. "Can I touch it?" he asked.

I pulled back. "No!" I said. I quickly began closing my shirt.

"Smells funny," Anthony said. "Like—like—"

Like Silly Putty! I thought. Rats! Why hadn't I thought of . . . ?

"Like a hospital," Kevin said quickly.

"Nah." Anthony wrinkled his forehead, trying to remember what the smell was.

"It's the glue," I said. "They use a special glue. I've noticed it, too, sometimes." Should I say it smells like Silly Putty—just in case they thought of it? Or should I just leave it?

"Glue?" Ryan said. "They use *glue*?"

Mistake! They were all looking at me.

I sighed and shook my head as if they were just too stupid. "Not glue like in paper glue," I said. "It's different. They sew everything on, but then they—they use glue to—to—"

"To close the skin," Kevin said.

"Right," I said. "To close the skin."

"It must have hurt a lot," Anthony said.

I shrugged. "Well, it was a long time ago."

"How long?" Greg asked.

I didn't answer. I wasn't going to, either. Weird how one lie could lead you into others.

I finished buttoning my shirt and then zipped my jacket. But Greg wouldn't let go of the question. "How long ago?" he asked again.

"Leave her alone, will you?" Brant said. He moved

It was hard to keep a straight face, but I realized nobody was looking at my face anyway, only at my neck.

in next to me, like he was protecting me from the rest of them. He looked serious, too, like I had honestly had my head cut off, and he really didn't want them to bother me.

I almost had to laugh. Brant is weird, but he can be cool, too, the way he really seems to care about people. I wondered if Miss Holt would ever love him back.

Greg shrugged, but he didn't ask the question anymore. And all seven of us went into school then. And I thought—*just four more days till Friday, election day*. And I had just tied up four more votes.

Later in the morning when it was our writing time, Miss Holt had us doing letters again—thank-you letters this time. I decided to send a reminder letter to the President. He'd probably completely forgotten. I wasn't sure I really needed his letter anymore, as long as those mystery people still voted for me. But I might as well try, just in case.

As usual, though, I couldn't let Miss Holt read it. So I had to write two letters—the real one to mail and one to show her, because we had to let her read our letters before we mailed them. Except that I mailed one after school one day, and she never even knew. The one I brought up for her to read was short—one paragraph. I thanked the President for sending me information about elections, even though he hadn't. And I asked him for his autograph. Then I went back and sat down to write the real letter. But when I went back to my seat, I noticed that half the people in the class were staring at me. No, they weren't staring at me; they were staring at my *neck*.

The Copycats hadn't told, had they?

I sat down and looked around the classroom. Was I imagining it?

Nope. At least half the kids were staring at me. But

they all looked away when I looked back. Except Owen. He just kept right on staring, his mouth hanging open like always.

I made a face back at him, letting my jaw drop open just like his. But he didn't seem to even notice that I was making fun of him. He even smiled at me.

I couldn't believe this! I looked at Kevin to see if he noticed, but he was busy writing his letter. And when I looked around the classroom again, nobody was looking at me anymore.

Yes. One was. Janie. Looking right at my neck, at my shirt. Then I remembered: I always wore my sweatshirts. Always! I bet this was the first time anyone had seen me wear a regular blouse, especially this dress-up kind. Maybe that's all it was!

Boy, what a bunch of stuck-up kids! Caring that much about what you wore. Didn't they know sweatshirts were the most comfortable clothes? I wore them all the time, to sleep in and everything. I'd even wear them to church if Ms. Henderson would let me.

But I was relieved that was all it was. At least, I was pretty sure that was it because I'd hate to have to try to fake out everyone in the class at once. Besides, knowing Janie, I realized she'd make a big deal out of saying it wasn't true. And I didn't want to take the chance of someone finding out it wasn't and of losing all my sure votes.

I reached up to scratch my neck. I couldn't wait to get rid of the scar. It was getting absolutely stiff. As soon as we had lavatory time, I was going to get in there and take it off. But it had been worth it—four more votes. Almost enough to win, if I got my mystery votes.

For now, though, I had to write my letter to the President, just in case.

When we finished our letters, Miss Holt said to get in line for gym. The boys always line up together and the girls together, even though there's no rule that says we have to. Even Kevin and I don't usually line up together, even though we're best friends outside school. But this time, Kevin got in line right behind me.

"How's your neck?" he said quietly.

"It's killing me," I answered. "I can't wait to get to the lavatory."

"Don't take it off," Kevin said, still very quietly. "Not yet."

I just looked at him. "Why?"

"You know how Anthony's in love with Violet?" he said.

"Yeah?"

"So he told her. And he said she could look at it."

"What?" I said it so loud that I saw Miss Holt frown at me.

He nodded and looked depressed.

"Well, she can't," I said.

"She'll vote for you."

"I don't care. I'm not showing. If she sees it, that means Janie'll want to see it. And if Janie knows, I'm in trouble."

Kevin sighed. "You're in trouble," he said.

11

"SHE KNOWS?" I said.

"She knows," Kevin answered.

"How do you know she knows?"

"Anthony told me."

"I'll get him," I said.

I was so mad. I'd get even with Anthony. But what was I going to do about Janie and Violet?

Before I could figure it out, though, we were at the door to the gym. We lined up in a row and got real silent, like a bunch of convicts or something. That's the way Miss Lizardo, the gym teacher, makes us come into the gym. It's one of her rules. She has about a hundred of them, and she keeps making up new ones to fit whenever she wants. When you ask her why about something, she always says, "Because that's Miss Lizardo's rule."

That's another weird thing about her—she talks about herself as if she wasn't there. She says things like, "Didn't Miss Lizardo tell you not to do that?" Or, "Miss Lizardo does not like the behavior in this class."

On the first day of school, she made everyone practice her name. We had to say "Lizardo" over and over, emphasizing the *zar* part. I know why she does that—so people won't call her "Lizard-o." But of course that's what everybody calls her anyway. At least, behind her back. That, or "Oh! Lizard!" She even looks like a lizard. Her hands are like claws, and her face is brown and wrinkled up.

We filed into the gym, and I looked across at Violet. She was next to Janie, and both of them were whispering and looking at me. What was I going to do now? Show them? No way. Janie'd figure it out. Or else tell the teachers, who'd figure it out. Janie looks dumb, but she's not. But then if I didn't show it to her, she'd say I was a liar.

"Line up, line up!" Miss Lizardo was shouting. "And remember Miss Lizardo's rule—silence! Now, boys on one side, girls on the other."

That meant kickball or mat ball—boys against the girls. I'm good at both of them. I hoped I'd get to be near Janie. I'd kick the ball right in her eye. Then she wouldn't be able to see my scar—or anything else.

All the girls were clumped up together, like a herd of sheep or something. As soon as Miss Lizardo said to line up, Violet grabbed Janie's arm so they could be together in line. There was a shoving match to see who could get on Janie's other side.

Since I couldn't be in line with Kevin, I looked around for some girl I didn't mind being next to. The only one standing alone, seeming not even to care, was Jennifer. Jennifer's real quiet, and I never know just what's going on inside her. I think she's nice, even though I really can't tell since she doesn't say anything. But she doesn't side with Janie all the time like all the rest of the girls. And she doesn't hang around in the pack. I wondered if she was one of the mystery ones who voted for me.

"Line *up!*" Miss Lizardo yelled again.

Very casually, I managed to get beside Jennifer.

Jennifer didn't even look at me when I came over, but as soon as I was next to her, she leaned in close. "Lookit her teeth," she whispered. "You ever see such long ones?"

It was the first time she'd ever spoken to me that I didn't speak first.

I nodded and whispered back, "And yellow."

" 'Cept for the two over to the sides. Brown."

"Yeah." She was right. I thought I was the only one who noticed stuff like that. Miss Lizardo's middle two teeth are long and yellow. But the two teeth on either side of the big ones, the ones that are sharp, sort of like dog teeth—those dog teeth are brown.

"Are we all ready now?" Miss Lizardo called out.

"Uh-oh," Jennifer whispered. "Cootie check." She nodded at a table set up in front near the basketball hoop.

I looked. There was a table and two chairs in the front, and the nurse, Miss Puckey, was there, too, with charts and stuff. They had a little screen set up by the one chair for privacy, but you could still see everything.

I sighed. What a boring thing to do with gym time! I hadn't had a cootie check since I was in first grade. It's what they do when even one kid in the whole school gets bugs in their hair. Then they check the whole entire school because they say bugs are catching.

"Rats!" I said. "Rats!" I had hoped for kickball and a chance to get Janie.

"Boring!" Jennifer muttered.

I nodded, but I didn't answer because Lizard was looking our way. I wished I could talk or whisper the way Jennifer does. She has a way of talking so that her mouth hardly moves at all. I wondered if you could learn that by practice or if it was something you were born with.

"Bet Lizard is the one who started it," Jennifer whispered. "She probably got the first bug."

Again I nodded. I scratched my neck. Talk about bugs! I hadn't had a chance to get to the lavatory, and my neck was itching as if I had a thousand bugs.

Jennifer was whispering again, but Lizard was looking at somebody else by then. "In third-grade gym," Jennifer whispered, "Miss Lizardo made us get undressed to get weighed. Right down to our underwear."

"In front of the boys?" I said.

"No. Separately. And the day she did that, I was wearing an undershirt. Janie was wearing a bra."

"In *third* grade?" I said.

Jennifer nodded and giggled.

"I wouldn't get undressed," I said.

"We don't have to anymore."

"Good thing."

Miss Lizardo was standing in the middle of the gym, hands at her sides. But she was pleating and unpleating her sweatpants as though she was nervous. "Now boys and girls," she said. "I'm afraid I don't like this any more than you do. But there have been one or two cases of—of—"

She looked at the nurse, as if she couldn't bring herself to say the word. "Of—"

"Head lice," said Miss Puckey, without looking up. "We'll start, first a boy, then a girl, then a boy, etcetera. Till we're finished. Let's start!"

She signaled to the first boy in line—Anthony.

If I could have given him head lice just then, I would have. Why did he have to go tell Violet? And Janie.

Anthony sat down at the desk behind the screen. Miss Puckey stood over him and combed through his hair.

Gross. We weren't supposed to be able to see because of the screen. But the screen was just made out of a thin sheet, and the nurse had a bright lamp on, so you could see right through it. Everybody just stood there watching, as though it was all done on wide-screen TV or something.

How dumb!

I leaned against the wall. I wondered what Miss Puckey would do if she found bugs on somebody. And if she did, and bugs were catching, wouldn't they get on her?

She finished with Anthony, then went on to the first girl—Stephanie. Stephanie has long hair, so it took longer. The nurse looked at her scalp, and then all through her hair, combing down all the way to the bottom. Then she lifted Stephanie's hair and looked under it, at the back of her scalp and neck.

I let out a big breath. This was going to take forever. At least they could have let us bring down a book or something to read.

Owen was going up front next.

"Who do you think's gonna have 'em?" Jennifer asked quietly, still without moving her lips.

I looked around at everybody, thinking. Everyone in the class looked pretty clean. But clean sometimes didn't have anything to do with who got bugs. I knew who I wished would have them: Anthony. Or Janie. They probably wouldn't, though. Life wasn't fair.

I shrugged and scratched my neck. I could feel the scar getting all bunched up into a ball, but it didn't matter now.

"Owen?" Jennifer whispered.

"Nah," I said. "Probably Miss Puckey."

"The nurse?" Jennifer laughed right out loud, and it

was so sudden, so surprising, that I couldn't help laughing, too.

Jennifer clamped her hand over her mouth, and her face got all red, but she went right on laughing.

And suddenly, I couldn't stop laughing, either.

Everybody turned around and looked at us, including, of course, Lizard.

She came right over to separate us. She put a hand on my shoulder and pushed me to the front of the line and pointed Jennifer to the back. "You know what Miss Lizardo's rules are," she said.

I went up to the front of the line, but I was still laughing. I stood right in front of Violet. She made a face at me, but I just shrugged. Could I help it? It was Miss Lizardo's fault. Actually, I didn't mind. At least I'd get it over with in a hurry. Then maybe I could get excused to go to the lavatory and get rid of the Silly Putty.

As soon as Owen was finished, I went up and sat down.

Miss Puckey bent over me and examined my head, scraping my scalp with a fine-toothed comb. Then she combed through my hair, from the top right down to the bottom.

I said "Ouch!" good and loud. But she kept right on going. It didn't really hurt that much, but I didn't like it at all. This was *my* hair, *my* head. Grown-ups didn't have any right to do things like this to kids. I wondered how they'd feel if we did this to them. Maybe I should tell Miss Puckey when she finished that I wanted to check out her head.

"All right, Bailey," she said. "That's fine. Now just hold up your hair and let me see your neck."

I held up my hair, though I knew there wasn't much of my neck that you could see. I had the shirt buttoned so high over the scar that it looked like I hardly had a neck at all. But it would just have to do.

Miss Puckey didn't think so, though. "Would you unbutton your collar so I can see your neck, please?" she said. "Just the top button is all."

"No," I said.

"Yes."

"No."

She sighed. "Bailey, this is silly. Now let me see your neck. We're only checking. You'll be finished in a minute."

I could feel everyone in the class watching and listening to me. Big-screen TV. There wasn't a sound. Nobody was even whispering or anything.

"It's *my* neck," I said. "*My* hair." I said it quietly, between clenched teeth. It *was* my neck. It *was* my hair. It wasn't anybody's business what my neck looked like.

Miss Puckey sighed.

Out of the corner of my eye, I could see Lizard moving in.

They weren't going to hold me down and unbutton my shirt, were they? Never. Or would they?

Both of them were standing over me now.

I looked from one to the other. Let them send me to the office. I didn't care. On the way there, I'd take off the scar. And then they could look at my neck all they wanted.

But Miss Puckey said, "All right, Bailey. It's your choice. This is your responsibility." She looked at me, then at Miss Lizardo. And then she said, "The entire class will wait here till you've made up your mind to cooperate. There will be no recess or free time until you do." She said it really loud, pronouncing each word separately and distinctly.

So much for privacy!

Everybody started groaning.

I looked toward Kevin and Brant. Brant looked kind of sick. So did Kevin.

I looked at Jennifer, but she wasn't looking back.

I waited, and waited, and waited.

They waited. And waited. And waited.

"Okay," I said at last. I knew I couldn't win this one. But I didn't have to show them the whole thing. I unbuttoned the top button of my shirt, and pulled it down just the tiniest, tiniest bit.

But Miss Puckey grabbed hold of my shirt collar and pulled it away from my neck, pulling it so far out in the back that she was choking me in front.

"Your neck is very red," she said.

"Yes," I said. "It always is."

"It looks quite irritated."

Yeah! The whole class was listening! *It was the head transplant that did it,* I thought. I willed the thought into everybody's head.

"Yes," I said quietly. "It gets that way sometimes."

"Have you been scratching?"

"No!" No way was I going to let them think I was scratching because I had cooties. "No," I said. "It just gets irritated from . . . from something else. From something a long time ago."

"Bailey?" Miss Puckey said. She sounded as if she was laughing. "Bailey, what is this?"

"What?" But instantly I knew what she was talking about.

She ran her finger down inside my shirt collar, fingering the Silly Putty that was all in a ball by then.

I jerked away. "It's nothing!" I said.

But just like that she figured it out. Instantly. Was it the smell that gave it away? Or because it was all balled up? She laughed, and then she said, "Bailey! What are you doing with Silly Putty on your neck?"

12

FOR THE NEXT three days, everybody teased and made jokes whenever they saw me. Kevin and Brant didn't, of course, but practically everybody else did. Even Jennifer, although she didn't laugh, acted as though she'd forgotten that she'd ever spoken to me.

At first, whenever anyone said something about how I shouldn't lose my head or something, I just laughed. Then I said, "Ha! Tricked you!" And pretended they weren't bothering me at all.

But they were. Not that I cared what they said. But I was pretty sure I'd lost votes, especially the Copycats' votes. And maybe I'd lost the mystery people, too. So I came up with an idea: I kept making excuses to go to the lavatory or the library or somewhere to hide out. I figured if people couldn't find me to tease me, maybe by Friday when the elections came, they'd have forgotten all about it.

It was Thursday, almost three o'clock, right before the dismissal bell rang, and I was in the lavatory in one of the stalls, when a whole bunch of girls came in. I recognized their voices right away—Marcia, Stephanie, Violet, and Janie. They didn't know I was there because I was in the handicapped stall in the far corner, the one I like. It's big and it has bars, and you can swing on them. I'd been in there a lot that day, just swinging back and forth.

As soon as I heard Janie and her gang come in, I lifted myself from the bars onto the toilet seat so they wouldn't see my feet. Then I peeked out and watched them through the crack in the door.

All four of them lined up in front of the mirror.

Janie took a blue hairbrush out of her purse and began brushing her hair. Marcia and Stephanie and Violet took out hairbrushes, too. *Blue* hairbrushes. And all four of them began brushing. They reminded me exactly of four monkeys.

Violet looked at Janie in the mirror. "Nobody'll vote for her now," she said.

"You'll get elected, Janie," Stephanie said.

"Yeah," Janie said. "I will."

"It was sort of a funny joke, though," Marcia said.

Everybody got quiet. Even if I wasn't watching through the crack, I'd have known just what was happening: Janie was giving one of those *looks* to Marcia, those chop-you-up-until-you're-dead looks. And the other girls were looking nervous.

"Uh, I mean," Marcia said, "I mean—it was funny that she thought she could trick people like that. That she thought anybody would believe her."

"Yeah," Janie said. "My father says that people like her do stuff like that. Instead of just working hard on getting votes, on *earning* votes—or earning anything— they just try to trick people."

"People like her?" Marcia said.

"You know," Janie answered. "People on welfare. Lazy people." Then she whispered something, and the whole bunch of them laughed.

I didn't know what she had whispered. But I knew it was ugly and mean.

They giggled some more, then put away their identical hairbrushes, and left. For a minute, I thought about following them out and telling them off. But I decided not to. Suddenly I had this awful feeling that Violet was right—that I couldn't win now.

I could hardly stand to think about it. But my mind wouldn't *not* think about it, either, just like happened in bed at night. If I didn't win, if I couldn't prove that the kids liked me, then Miss Rothbart, the social worker, would move me. I was sure of that now. I wondered if she had come to school yet to talk to Miss Holt. Social workers always came to check up on you. If she had, she'd find out how few friends I really had. I did have other friends besides school friends, though—like my homeless friend Jessica, who lives on Spruce Street. But I guess to someone like Miss Rothbart, Jessica, a street person, wouldn't count.

There was another reason, though, that I didn't follow Janie and tell her off right then—a bigger reason. It was because she was right. I mean, I knew she was a jerk, but she was right about one thing: I hadn't worked hard enough on earning votes. But how did you *earn* votes? By being good enough. By being the kind of person somebody wanted. And I wasn't sure that I was that kind of person at all, the kind that people wanted. I'd always been the kind that nobody wanted.

Suddenly—it was so dumb!—I felt as though I was going to cry. No! I shook my head hard and blinked fast. Think about something, something funny—Brant being in love with Miss Holt. The joke I'd played on Janie. Shakespeare.

Nothing worked. I was crying.

I never cry! I had to get out of there. I didn't even wait for the bell to ring, and I didn't go to the classroom for my books or anything. I just grabbed my coat from the hall locker and raced outside to the bike rack. When I got there, I heard the bell ringing, and I quickly unlocked my bike. I didn't want to see anyone, not even Kevin or Brant.

I hopped on my bike and took a different way home from the usual—by way of Spruce Street. That is the ugly part of town where all the street people live, and none of the kids ever goes there. None of the kids but me.

As soon as I got on my bike, I felt a lot better, just like I knew I would. I rode super fast, feeling the wind rush against my face. Everything was going to be all right. If I had to move, I'd move. No big deal. I'd done it lots of times before.

As I was heading toward Spruce Street, I was thinking about the homeless people who live there. Suddenly, I remembered something that Jessica had told me one day about street people. It was a really cold day, just like today. The police had come and were trying to move the homeless people into shelters. Some of them didn't want to go. Jessica had walked up to the policeman and kept him so busy talking that the ones who didn't want to go had a chance to sneak away.

Afterward, Jessica had grinned at me. And that's when she'd said it. "We're free as the wind," she said.

Free as the wind, I thought.

There was something I had to ask her.

When I got to Spruce Street, I looked and found her on her usual corner. She was sitting scrunched up in a doorway, wrapped in an enormous greenish blanket, her feet hidden by a pile of newspapers. Her friend Dahlia was asleep in a big cardboard box behind her, all wrapped up in rags. I came to a stop in front of her—close to her, so I wouldn't hurt her feelings. She told me once that people always walk way far away from her because she smells. She does smell, too, but she can't help it. She has no place to go to wash.

She looked up at me, a mean, squinty-eyed, scary look. I looked right back at her. I know that she deliberately does that to scare off people sometimes. But she's always been friendly to me.

After a minute, she stopped giving me that mean look, and then she nodded. "What you want?"

I took a deep breath. "Jessica," I said, "if you didn't live here on the street, where would you live?"

"Don't live on no *street*," Jessica said. She reached behind her and patted her box. "I live in this *box*." She sounded so formal and proud that I wondered for the first time who she'd been before she'd become a street person.

I played with the string on my jacket hood. "Well," I said, "suppose I wanted to live here, too. Where could I live—if I didn't have a box to live in?"

Jessica looked over at Dahlia. "Mine don't have room for three," she said. She sounded sad.

For a second, I almost laughed. Then I realized that she really meant it—that if it was big enough, she'd share her box with me. Somebody wanted me.

"It's okay," I said, and I smiled.

But she was giving me her mean, squinty-eyed look again. "What you want to live on the street for?" she said. "You in trouble?"

I didn't need her acting like a hot-shot social worker. She's the one who told me—free, free as the wind, she'd said.

I made the same squinty-eyed look at her that she was giving to me. "None of your business," I said.

"Don't go doin' nothin' stupid," she said.

"Oh, shut up," I said.

She just kept staring at me. Then she shook her head, and her mean look went away and she almost smiled. "Kids is a mess," she said. She looked toward Dahlia in the box behind her. Then she added, kind of sadly, "Jus' like grown folk."

She sighed.

I sighed, too. "Yeah," I said. And then I said, "Well, bye, Jessica." And I got back on my bike and headed for Ms. Henderson's place.

Lots of things were a mess, I thought. But being a street kid probably wouldn't have worked, anyway. Still, it had been a good idea for a while. No more foster kid anymore. Just a regular kid. And like Jessica—free as the wind.

When I got home, I checked the mailbox the way I always do, just in case there was a letter from the President. But there was nothing, no mail at all. Not even an ad or a sample box of toothpaste.

I went upstairs and into the kitchen. Ms. Henderson was at the kitchen table, reading that dumb newspaper that got me in trouble. She looked up, surprised when I came in, probably because I was so early. Usually I don't get home until just before it's time to baby-sit Matt.

"Hi, sweetie!" she said.

"Hi." I went to the refrigerator for some milk. None as usual. The plastic container had about a dribble left in it. It was my job to make up the powdered stuff every day, and I always put off doing it. I hate powdered milk. It gets lumps in it no matter what I do.

I slammed the refrigerator door. Well, at least the next place I went, maybe I'd get real milk. I started for my room.

"Something wrong, sweetie?" Ms. Henderson called after me.

"Wrong?" I said. "Ha!" Real sarcastic. But what did she care? She sat reading stupid newspapers and not telling me what she was thinking. And all the while, probably planning with Miss Rothbart how to get rid of me.

I had to go through the living room to get to my room. As I did, I almost tripped and killed myself trying not to step on Matt, who was asleep, thumb in mouth, on the floor in front of the TV.

"Stupid place to sleep!" I shouted. No wonder he never wants to go to bed at night—she lets him sleep all afternoon.

I slammed my bedroom door.

Matt woke up, crying. There. That made me feel a little better.

I went to my closet and pulled out my suitcase. I'd be all packed when they came to move me. I'd tell them that I was dying to leave—had gotten ready before they even thought of it.

But before I opened my suitcase, I stopped, thinking. I knew what I would find in there—Shakespeare, my bear. I opened the suitcase and took Shakespeare out. His nose is almost gone from kissing him so much, and one of his eyes is missing. It fell off a long time ago, and once I sewed a button on instead because I thought he'd want two eyes. But the button made him look funny—he didn't look like Shakespeare anymore. So I took it off again, and I think he likes it better that way. After I fluffed up his fur a little, I set him on the bed while I packed.

In about five minutes, I was all done except for the stuff I was going to wear to school tomorrow.

The only other thing I didn't pack yet was Shakespeare. I figured he needed some air since he'd been in the suitcase for so long. I lay down on the bed for a minute, hugging him while I thought for a while.

It was cold in my room, and I pulled the covers tight around me. I must have fallen asleep because the next thing I knew, someone was knocking on my door.

I sat up, startled, and threw the covers off. They had gotten tangled all around my legs, and I was hot. "What?" I said.

"You have to baby-sit me," Matt said through the closed door. "It's five o'clock."

"Okay," I said.

I got out of bed and looked around my room. I put the suitcase back under the bed and stuffed Shakespeare under my pillow so Matt wouldn't see him. Then I went out in the kitchen.

Matt was sitting at the table, making big, scribbly circles all over his coloring book, one different-colored circle on each page. Little kids sure don't care if they mess up their coloring books. At the same time that he was wrecking his bock, he was counting in Spanish.

Ms. Henderson was at the door, her coat and hat on. She looked at me, that weird, looking-over-my-shoulder look she has. "You were sleeping?" she asked.

I nodded.

"You look flushed," she said. Then she smiled. "Pretty," she said. And she left.

When she was gone, I went in the bathroom and looked in the mirror. Nobody had ever said I was pretty before. Was I pretty? I couldn't tell. How do you know if you are or not?

I shrugged and went back to the kitchen. Just when I got there, the door opened again and Ms. Henderson stuck her head in. "I forgot to tell you," she said. She

I lay down on the bed for a minute, hugging him while I thought for a while.

nodded to the counter over by the stove. "You got a letter today." And then she went out again.

A *letter*? My heart began beating like crazy.

I went to the counter and grabbed up the envelope lying there. A stiff white envelope addressed to me: Miss Bailey Natalia Wharton. My hands were shaking, so I couldn't open it. But I didn't even have to, to know who it was from. It said it right there on the outside, and I shouted when I saw it.

"I got it!" I shouted. "I got it!"

I ran to the phone to call Kevin, holding the letter tight against my chest—a letter I hadn't even opened yet. The letter that said: OFFICE OF THE PRESIDENT. THE WHITE HOUSE. WASHINGTON, D.C.

13

NEXT MORNING EARLY I was at Kevin's house, practically before the sun was up. We sat at the kitchen table, reading the letter over and over and over again. I had read it to him on the phone, but still we reread and reread. If you could wear out writing just by reading it, it would have been all gone by schooltime.

This is what it said:

Miss Bailey Natalia Wharton

Dear Bailey:

Thank you for your nice letter. Yes, I do know how it feels to run for president. And I know how important it is to win. However, I have much confidence in you because even though it's hard work to be a president, you seem to have the necessary skills. You know how to communicate and how to persuade others, and these are important leadership skills.

I'm very proud that you're learning about the election process and are willing to work and do a difficult job. I wish you all good luck.

By the way, I do have friends who are girls. But they don't all vote for me. And I think it would be a good idea for a woman to be president.

And it was signed with his name and then "Executive Office of the President of the United States."

"Man!" Kevin said, after we'd reread it for the zillionth time. "Wait'll they see this! And what timing with elections today."

I rewrapped the letter in the Saran Wrap I had put it in last night to keep it clean. I didn't answer right away because I knew when I told him what I was planning, he'd scream. But I was pretty sure it was the right thing to do. I'd been awake practically all night thinking about it.

Kevin got up and put two Poptarts in the toaster, one for him and one for me. "So?" he said. "You gonna put it on the bulletin board? Or make an announcement? Or what?"

"Don't know yet," I said.

"I can't wait to see Miss Holt's face," Kevin said. "And Janie's."

He brought the Poptarts back to the table and gave me one—Dutch apple, my favorite.

I bit into it and didn't look at him. "I'm not sure I'm going to show her," I said.

"Who? Janie?"

"Anybody."

"Huh?"

"Not yet, I mean," I said.

"When then?"

"After the elections."

"*After* the elections? What are you—weird?"

I didn't answer.

"But that's what you wanted it for!" Kevin said. "So you could win!" He was staring at me over his Poptart, as if I had just lost my mind.

I shrugged.

"Why?" Kevin said. "Because the President didn't say that kids should vote for you? That doesn't matter. You know they will when they see it."

I shook my head. "It's not that. It's just that—that maybe I don't want to win that way."

"What do you mean, 'that way'? *What* way?" He sounded as though he was about to scream.

I sighed. It was hard to talk about, hard to tell him why I shouldn't use the letter. Hard to tell him what Janie had said the other day. That I didn't earn votes. That her father had said that people like me didn't earn anything. Because that was the reason I didn't want to use the letter. I wouldn't *earn* votes that way. If I showed the letter, it would be to impress the kids, to make kids vote for me. And that was no way to earn a vote.

Kevin was still staring at me, waiting. I didn't want to say these things to him, but I knew it wouldn't be fair not to.

"I'll tell you on the way to school," I said.

I brushed off the crumbs and stood up. Then I put the letter inside my notebook.

We both got our coats on and started for school. It was really freezing that day, so neither of us wanted to ride our bikes.

As we walked, I told him what Janie had said. The whole thing—about me being lazy and being on welfare and not earning votes and everything.

"So what?" Kevin said after I finished. "Janie's a jerk."

"I know," I said. "But even jerks are right sometimes."

"Not this time," he said.

I looked at him.

"I mean it," he said. He sounded weird—fierce or mad or something.

We had gotten to school, and we sat down on the steps. It was freezing sitting there like that, but we were so early the janitor hadn't arrived yet, and school was still all locked up.

Kevin began rubbing his sneaker against the steps, twisting a little piece of rubber loose from the edge of the sole. His face had gotten red as if he were embarrassed. But after a minute he took a big breath and looked up at me.

"Remember last fall?" he said. "When I was eating flies and spiders?"

I nodded and grinned. "And goldfish," I said. Because once he had even swallowed Miss Holt's fish—after it was dead, of course.

He nodded. "You know why I was doing that?"

"Why?"

"Because I needed to—I don't know. Show off or something. So people would think I was . . . you know."

I nodded. I did know.

"So you know why I stopped?" he said.

I shook my head no.

" 'Cause of you."

"*Me?*"

Kevin nodded, and now he looked even more embarrassed, but he went on. "See, you don't try to impress anyone. Or prove anything. Or dress up fancy. Or show off—"

"Yeah?" I said. "What about the scar?"

"That wasn't showing off," he said. "It was— You needed it for votes." Then he added, "I'm trying to tell you something. You're just *you*."

Now I felt embarrassed, even though it made me feel good. But I wasn't sure that what he was saying had anything to do with earning votes.

But Kevin obviously thought so. "See," he said. "You don't have to *earn* anything! That's what I'm trying to say. You're just you. And that's enough." Then, as if he had explained everything, he added, "So show them the letter."

I didn't think so, but I didn't want him to feel bad. So I just said, "Maybe."

Kevin shook his head. Together, we watched Mr. Luparello, the school janitor, come toddling up the walk. Mr. Luparello must be a hundred years old. He was squinting at us suspiciously—not too many people line up to get into school early.

Kevin stood up to help hold Mr. Luparello's stuff while he unlocked the doors. While he did that, I stood there watching and thinking. What was it Kevin was trying to tell me—that you didn't have to *earn* votes, that you didn't have to prove something? That all you had to do was be you? But that couldn't be right. Could it? Or maybe—maybe it was *partly* right?

When we got inside, Kevin and I went right to our classroom. Kevin was so excited, I wondered whether he could do it if I told him not to say anything about the letter.

We had just put away our books and hung up our coats when Miss Holt came in. "Good morning," she said. Even though she looked surprised, she didn't say anything else.

Kevin poked me.

I poked him back.

He poked me again.

I decided to ignore him.

Miss Holt sat down at the desk and poured herself some coffee from her thermos. She didn't look at us, but after a minute, she said, "So. Anything new?"

Again Kevin poked me.

I glared at him. I'd be black and blue if he didn't stop it. I kicked him under the desk.

And then Janie came rushing into the room, breathless. She stopped short when she saw Kevin and me, but turned to Miss Holt.

"Miss Holt!" she said. "Can I be excused early on Monday?" She waved an envelope. "I have a note from my mother. It's because of my grandmother."

I looked at Kevin. "The dead one?" I said.

Kevin laughed right out loud. But for once, Elephant Ears didn't hear. Or she decided to pretend she hadn't.

"She's coming here from Italy," Janie said. "And my father and mother want me to meet her at the airport with them. Oh, Miss Holt, could I? Could I leave early?"

"I don't see why not," Miss Holt said.

"Oh, good," Janie said, and she took a deep breath of relief. "And today is elections. Then when I meet my grandmother . . . I can tell her I'm president."

She quickly ducked her head then, like she was embarrassed, but you could see that she was smiling. "I mean," she said, "if I win."

But you could tell exactly what she meant—*when* I win.

Kevin started to poke me again, but I pulled my arm back away from him.

When the rest of the kids arrived, some of them still made some jokes about my head transplant, but most kids had pretty much gotten tired of joking on me. I had figured that would happen—people make a big thing of something for a while, and then they forget all about it.

And besides, everyone was too busy with something else—Janie.

She was going to each one's desk, bending down, and whispering—she even whispered to the boys. Then she gave each person a pencil with a tiny plastic bird attached to it by a spring. When you wrote, the little bird bobbled its head up and down, tapping against the pencil. On every single pencil were these words: VOTE FOR JANIE—FOR PRESIDENT!

I looked at Kevin. He made a face at Janie's back. "Follow her," he said quietly. "Go to each desk right after her and show the letter."

I shook my head no.

"You make me mad!" Kevin said.

"Tough," I said.

When everyone was in class, Miss Holt made an announcement. "If you would all please get in your seats and settle down," she said. "We'll be having elections this morning. And it's time for our campaign speeches."

People slid into their seats, but there was a lot of talking. I had sort of forgotten about the speeches. Not exactly forgotten, but I hadn't been thinking about them much because giving talks doesn't worry me. I knew I'd think of something to say, such as just telling kids to vote for me, that I'd be better than Janie any day. But suddenly I began thinking about Janie again and all that stuff about earning votes. What could I say about that? Had I earned any votes?

Janie leaned over and put one of her bird pencils on my desk.

I pushed it back at her.

She just shrugged, and I saw her smile at Violet.

"Now, class," Miss Holt said, after everyone had settled down. "The election process is an important one. I know that, during campaigns, sometimes promises are made . . . "

I felt half the class looking at me.

I reached over and snatched a pencil off Janie's desk— a bird pencil. I pretended to be playing with it, but I held it up in front of my face, making sure everyone saw it. *Promises?* I thought. How about *bribes?*

Miss Holt went on, "But after all the promises and all the talk and all the little favors, you must vote for the candidate whose qualities you think are most important. The one who has the strength to lead. Maybe the one who is tough . . . "

She looked at me for just a moment. Then she looked away, took out the little shoe box that she uses as a ballot box, and put it on her desk.

"Now," she said, "I would like to give the candidates an opportunity to say a final word about their candidacy. And then we'll vote." She smiled. "Janie? Will you begin?"

Janie came up front and stood next to Miss Holt's desk. Her face got real red, the way it does when she has to give a talk, but she sure wasn't shy. Right away she started to brag. "I think you should vote for me," she said, "because *I'd* be a good president. *I'm* a good student. *I* get straight *A*'s. *I'm* a leader. *I've* lived here a long time—"

She paused, and for just a second her eyes flicked over me, as though she was going to say, "Not like some people." But she didn't.

She just went on. "I've gone to this school ever since kindergarten so I know what the kids here want. *I* know how to use computers, and *I* could do things on the computer that the class would need—I could even write a class newspaper on the computer."

She began rocking, the way she does when she gives a report, up on her toes and then down. You could see her really warming up to this. "And *I* know many different things—different cultures. And I'm learning to speak different languages, like Italian and Latin."

I rolled my eyes at Kevin, and he did it back. Just what we needed—a class president who could speak Latin.

Miss Holt leaned over and whispered something to Janie.

Janie nodded, and she said, "That's all." But then she looked right at me with her slimy smile. "Except you should vote for me because I've worked hard at *earning* your votes." Then she went and sat down.

"Thank you, Janie," Miss Holt said. "Bailey?"

She gave me that funny look she does sometimes. I remembered the day she first announced the elections, and how I got the feeling that she wanted me to run. Why? Maybe because she thought I'd be strong or tough? She had given me that quick look before—when she said that thing about being tough.

I hadn't any idea what she was thinking now. But she looked serious and interested, as if she cared and was waiting to hear what I'd say.

I stood up. I realized I didn't have any idea at all what to say. I saw Kevin looking at me hard, and I could tell he thought he knew what I should say—that I got a letter from the President.

I came up to the front of the room. I didn't stand by Miss Holt's desk. But Brant's desk was in the front, so I stood by his—for courage.

I looked out over the class. I guess Miss Holt's serious look was catching. Lots of people were looking back at me with very serious looks, not like they were laughing or teasing about my head transplant, but just like they were waiting to hear what I'd say.

"I would like you to vote for me," I said.

I couldn't think of one other thing to say because suddenly, as I stood there, the whole election thing seemed more important than ever. I thought of Ms. Henderson and Matt and how I needed—wanted—to stay here. Yes, I did want that. They weren't at all the kind of family I'd always dreamed of getting—a real mother and a father, too. But they were okay. And the kids here were mean, some of them. But there was Kevin and Brant and maybe even Jennifer. And some other kids I didn't know who had voted for me. And even Miss Holt, who seemed to want me. I wanted to stay.

I had to say something, so I took a deep breath and began.

"Janie said she earned your votes," I said. "She probably did. She worked really hard."

I looked at her. She looked as surprised as if she had just swallowed a bird or something. Her mouth hung open just like Owen's does. I almost laughed out loud. But I didn't because—I don't know—I guess because I meant it. Even if she was a jerk, she had worked hard.

"Anyway," I went on, "I'm not sure I earned your votes, because—well, because I don't know how to earn votes."

People looked surprised, but nobody was laughing at me. Kevin looked absolutely stunned. But at the same time, I could tell from his face that he was proud of me. So I got a little more courage.

"So," I said, "you just have to decide if you want me for a president, if you think I'll do a good job. Or if you want Janie, if you think she'll do a better job. As Miss

121

Holt said, you have to decide who has the qualities you want."

I turned to look at Miss Holt. "Who has strength. Or is tough. Right?"

Miss Holt nodded. "Right," she said softly.

I turned back to the class. I grinned. I couldn't help it. I was tough, I knew that. Tough enough to say the rest.

"I can do some pretty dumb things, can't I?" I said.

Everybody laughed. Janie laughed loudest, but I didn't care. I knew most of the kids weren't really laughing *at* me. Maybe even Janie wasn't, either.

"But I can do some pretty smart things, too," I said. "So you have to decide. If you want me, vote for me, if you think I'm the one for the job. If you want Janie, vote for Janie."

I smiled at the kids, most of whom were smiling back at me. I said, "So you have to choose . . . "

Again Ms. Henderson and Matt came into my mind. And Miss Rothbart and the letter from the President. Even Jessica and being free like the wind. Choices, so many choices. And I wanted to say, choose me because I've chosen to be here. But I couldn't.

It was time to finish. So I said, "Vote for me if you think I'll do the best job. Or for Janie if you think she'll be best."

Then I had to say the rest because it was true. "But I'll do a better job," I said.

And then I went back and sat down.

14

FOR THE NEXT five minutes, all you could hear was the clacking of little plastic birds against Janie's pencils as everybody wrote down their choice for president.

But did we get to find out who won? No. We had to wait the whole rest of the day because Miss Holt said she wouldn't announce the decision until the end of the day. I thought that was pretty mean. How could you do any work, wondering whether your life had just changed or not? Maybe to Janie it didn't make that much difference, but it sure did to me.

The day seemed as long as the day before Christmas. But finally, just before three o'clock, Miss Holt had us all sit down. We had our coats on and everything—all ready to go. I don't know why she did it that way, unless it was because she wanted whoever lost to have the chance to just get out of there in a hurry—probably she knew Janie would cry. Or was she afraid I'd cry? Maybe she did know how important it was.

After we were all seated and quiet, Miss Holt began. "Now, class," she said. "No matter who has won or who has lost, this has been a good experience for the entire class."

She had her serious face on, and I sighed. A lecture

was coming, I could tell. I looked at my watch. Well, she could only talk for five minutes, anyway. Buses got called at 3:05.

"The election process is important to the American system, as you all know . . . "

I wanted to raise my hand and say, "Will you just tell us who won?"

But before I could, an announcement came over the P.A. "Bus 57! Riders for bus 57 will be excused, please."

"Oh!" Miss Holt said. She looked at her watch. "It's later than I thought."

The kids for bus 57 got up and headed for the door. Jennifer was the first one in line. "But who won, Miss Holt?" she said.

Miss Holt looked at Janie. "Janie," she started to say. "Janie—"

"Janie?" Jennifer said. "*Janie?*" She practically wailed it like she was about to cry.

So was I.

Janie was already smiling her slimy smile.

"No!" Miss Holt said. "No! I'm sorry. I didn't mean to confuse you. You especially, Janie. What I started to say was, Janie, I'm sorry. You lost—not by much—but you lost."

"I lost?" Janie said. "*I* lost?"

Miss Holt nodded. "I'm afraid so."

Miss Holt turned to me then. "And you, Bailey." She smiled, a sweet smile. "Congratulations."

I nodded, but I couldn't answer.

My mind was full of jumble. I won! I won!

Janie's gang surrounded her. Some of them looked scared, as if they knew she was going to be mad at them. And all of them were sad-looking and silent.

But there was a lot of noise around me. A bunch of

kids rushed over to congratulate me—Kevin and Brant and Robby and Owen and Donald and even the Copycats. They weren't mad or making fun of me anymore. Even Jennifer raced back from the door and said, "Yay!"

I said thank you, but I couldn't really think of what else to say. So many kids had voted for me. So many kids wanted me! I really thought for a minute that I would start to cry. But of course I didn't.

The rest of the buses were called, and then the walkers. As soon as walkers were called, Kevin and Brant and I raced out of there. I had to go in a hurry because Janie looked so sad that I was beginning to feel bad for her.

Once outside, Kevin said, "This is so great! Awesome! And I thought for a minute—"

"Me, too," I said.

"Not me," Brant said. "Miss Holt was feeling sorry for Janie. You can tell just by looking at her face exactly what she's thinking."

"*You* can," I said. "That's 'cause you're in love." But I didn't say it in a mean way.

"Yup." Brant nodded and looked happy.

I smiled at him.

"You gonna show the letter now?" Kevin asked. "Monday?"

"Yup," I said. "Now that we won. And we never did have to get Sarah a horse or Jennifer a kitten."

"Yeah," Brant said. "I bet Jennifer voted for you anyway."

"We still have to do papers for Robby this Sunday," Kevin said.

"Who cares?" I said. "We won!"

"Want to do something this afternoon?" Kevin said. He grinned. "Now that we can stop campaigning?"

"Sure," I said. "But in a little while, okay?" Because

125

I realized that I had something else to do—something important.

We were at the corner where we separate. "See you in a little while," I said. I left them there and ran the whole rest of the way home.

I raced up the stairs in my lucky way—skipping the broken fourth step and then the eighth step, too.

When I came in, Ms. Henderson was sitting at the kitchen table, reading her weird newspaper. Matt was wrecking his coloring book with big circles again.

Ms. Henderson looked up. "Hi, sweetie," she said.

"*Buenos días,*" Matt said. He looked very proud of himself.

"Hi," I said.

For some reason, I felt shy. I had thought I'd come in and tell all about the election, that I was president. Instead I just felt tongue-tied. How weird!

I went to the refrigerator for some milk. As usual, there wasn't any, so I took the container over to the sink to make up the powdered stuff. I was glad to do it, though, because it gave me a chance to think. Why couldn't I just tell them about it? It's what I had come here to do.

"How was your day?" Ms. Henderson asked, in that vague kind of way.

"I won the election!" I turned around from the sink and blurted it out like—like I don't know what. But I was so excited I practically couldn't say it, even more excited than I had felt at school. "I won!" I said. "Me!"

"You did!" Ms. Henderson said. She smiled at me, not that vague smile but a really big, ordinary, regular smile. And the way she looked at me, she even seemed able to focus her eyes better so that she was looking practically straight at me.

"I'm glad," she said. "I'm so glad!"

A bunch of kids rushed over to congratulate me.

She got up from the table, and for a minute I thought she was going to hug me. I stepped back. I mean—I wasn't sure I wanted that.

But I guess that wasn't what she was going to do at all because she just came over to the sink. "There's something for you in the freezer," she said. She took the milk container from me and went to work on the powdered milk herself. "Go look."

I crossed the kitchen and opened the top part of the refrigerator, the freezer part.

It was packed—*packed full*—with boxes and boxes and boxes of frozen macaroni and cheese. There must have been fifty boxes in there!

I turned around to her. "For me?" I said. And knew it was a stupid question.

Ms. Henderson nodded. "For winning. I was pretty sure you'd win."

"But there's so many here!" I said.

"Well," Ms. Henderson said, "you're going to be here for a long time." Quickly she turned away, facing the sink, her back to me. When she spoke again, that other voice was back, the vague and dreamy one that sounded as if she hardly cared. "I mean you'll be here a while—if you want to be here. That's up to you."

Just like that I realized: She does that on purpose, that vague stuff. It's because if she sounds that way, no one can know she cares. And she does care. Why else would she have done this?

Still, even though I knew I wanted to stay here, still I wanted her to say it first.

I was still holding the door of the freezer that was packed with macaroni and cheese. Suddenly, I felt tears come to my eyes. Macaroni and cheese, a gift from Ms. Henderson who didn't have money to buy fifty boxes of frozen macaroni and cheese. Except that somehow she had gotten it because she cared . . .

I swallowed hard, and forced my voice to come out normal. "Of course I want to stay here," I said.

"Yay!" Matt yelled. It was the first thing he had said since he'd said, "*Buenos días.*" He looked at Ms. Henderson. "I told you so!" he said. "I told you so!"

She turned from the sink, and she looked right at me again. "I'm glad," she said, not at all vague-sounding or dreamy. "I want you to stay."

"But what about Miss Rothbart?" I said, suddenly scared. "The social worker? Can she make me leave?"

"*Her?*" Ms. Henderson said. She said it as though she couldn't be bothered with Miss Rothbart. "She's been here a couple times, trying to decide if I could get a permanent license or not. She wasn't going to give it to me just because of the electric bill." She smiled again and reached for her purse that was on the chair and took something out. "But I got it anyway. I called up her superior. I have this letter." She held it out to show me.

I didn't read it, but I saw that it was from Social Services. Suddenly I had a thought: I didn't have to win the election to stay here. I was going to stay anyway. But I did win—and found out the kids wanted me.

They wanted me, just like Ms. Henderson did.

She was smiling at me now, but she looked a little embarrassed, too. "I even told them you were class president now."

"Before today you told them that?"

She nodded.

I laughed.

She did, too. "I'm a licensed foster mother now," she said.

Licensed—you needed a license to keep a kid? Did real parents have licenses, too?

"I wanted it in writing so that no one could take you away from me," she said. "Not without a fight, they couldn't."

I was so surprised I couldn't answer. But then she surprised me even more.

"You have a strange and lovely way," she said softly. She smiled. "I didn't want to let you go."

I had to get out of that room. No way was I going to start bawling like a baby.

I went to my room and took my suitcase out from under the bed where I had hidden it. I unpacked it, taking out all the stuff I had just packed. When I was finished, I kissed Shakespeare, then put him back in the suitcase, and slid it under the bed again. But the minute I did, I instantly thought of something, and I pulled it back out again. I opened it, took Shakespeare out, and held him up to my face.

"Are you tired of living in a suitcase?" I said softly to him.

I made him nod his head yes.

"Me, too," I said. I set him on the bed. He looked good there.

By the time I had done all that, I didn't feel at all like crying anymore. I put on my coat. Kevin and Brant were waiting for me.

I went out in the kitchen again. Ms. Henderson and Matt were still at the table, Matt still scribbling all over his book and saying stuff in Spanish.

"*No se apoye contre la puerta*," he said when I came in to the kitchen.

"Where'd you learn that?" I said.

"On the subway. The bus, too."

"What's it mean?" I said.

" 'Do not lean against these doors,' " he said.

"A lot of good that'll do you," I said.

Then I looked at Ms. Henderson and thought of her words—words as unfamiliar to me as Matt's words. "I didn't want to let you go."

Suddenly, once again, I heard in my head the words I hear so often, the ones of the social worker, the one from long ago—"Nobody wants her." But this time, I almost laughed out loud.

Because it wasn't true. Not anymore it wasn't.

I went to Ms. Henderson and leaned over, not too close, not close enough for a hug or a kiss or anything, but just close enough for her to hear. "I'm glad you—" I said. But I stopped.

I didn't know the right words, the words that would say exactly what I meant. So I said the closest thing I could. "I mean," I said. "Thanks for the macaroni and cheese."

And then I got out of there and raced toward Kevin's house. Later, at five o'clock, when it was time to baby-sit Matt again, I'd come back. Back to Ms. Henderson's place. Back home.